D1577011

BRISTOL LIBRARIES
WITHDRAWN
SOLD AS SEEN

# CARS OF THE 50s

BY JAMES M. FLAMMANG
AND THE AUTO EDITORS OF CONSUMER GUIDE®

Publications International, Ltd.

Copyright © 2008 Publications International, Ltd. All rights reserved.
This book may not be reproduced or quoted in whole or in part by
any means whatsoever without written permission from:

Louis Weber, CEO
Publications International, Ltd.
7373 North Cicero Avenue
Lincolnwood, Illinois 60712

Permission is never granted for commercial purposes.

ISBN-13: 978-1-4127-7118-4
ISBN-10: 1-4127-7118-8

Manufactured in China.

8 7 6 5 4 3 2 1

Library of Congress Control Number: 2008926778

# Acknowledgements

**Chapter-Introduction Paintings:** Mitch Frumkin

**PHOTOGRAPHY**
The editors gratefully acknowledge the cooperation of the following people who supplied photography to help make this book possible.

Dan Lyons; Bud Davis, **Sunoco;** John M. Weir and Art Kistler, **Illinois Dept. of Transportation;** Dan Erickson, **Ford Photographic Services;** Leo Larkin, **Chicago Auto Trade Association;** Chan Bush; Bud Juneau; Ron McQueeney, **Indy 500 Photos;** Hampton Smith, **Minnesota Historical Society;** Barbara Fronczak and Brandt Rosenbush, **Chrysler Historical Society;** Helen Early and James R. Walkinshaw, **Oldsmobile History Center;** Milton Gene Kieft; Vince Mannochi; Linda Ziemer, **Chicago Historical Society;** Joseph Wherry; Richard Langworth; Sam Griffith; Brooks Stevens; Hub Willson; Debra Gust, **Curt Teich Postcard Archives, Lake County (IL) Museum;** Mike Mueller; Richard Quinn; Nicky Wright; Christopher Raab; **A&W Restaurants, Inc.;** Rick Blodgett; Christine J. Baker, **Pennsylvania Turnpike Commission;** Jack Markley and Mark McDonald **Illinois State Police;** Thomas Glatch; Steve Statham; Christina M. Purcell, **Cadillac Public Relations;** Lt. C. Gross, **Cicero Police Department;** John A. Conde Collection; Pat Witry, **Skokie Historical Society;** Mary M. Belen, **Michigan State Police;** Laura Toole, **Chevrolet Public Relations;** Daniel F. Kirchner and Peggy Dusman, **American Automobile Manufacturers Association;** Mary Keane, **Mobil Oil Corp.;** Bill Watkins; H. Russ Garrett; Rick Lenz; Joseph H. Wherry Collection; John Blake; Richard Spiegelman; Doug Mitchel; Bert Johnson; Lloyd Koening; **Houston Police Dept;** Laurel H. Kenney; Thomas A. Suszka, **New Jersey Turnpike Authority; Cinema Collectors;** Art Kistler, Kim Bartley, **White Castle System, Inc.;** Jim Frenak; Debbie Mason, **JM Family Enterprises;** Richard M. Langworth; Jean Denham, **Studebaker Museum;** Jim Thompson; David Gooley; Gary D.Smith; Fay Meek, **California Dept. of Transportation;** C. Thomas; Larry Gustin and David Roman, **Buick Public Relations;** Bill Kilborn; Jim Frenak; Jack C. Miller Collection; Jim Benjaminson; Terrell Photography; Bill Nichols and David G. Shirley, **Mitchell Corporation;** Joe Bohovic; Michael Brown; Eddie Goldberger; Jerry Heasley; Tom Storm; **Hawaii State Archives;** Robert Waggener; Ron McNicholl; Ron Moorhead; Linda Fontana, **McDonalds Corporation;** Scott Baxter; Tom Ernst; Elaine Richner, **Denny's Inc.;** Ted Clow; Steve Statham; D. Randy Riggs; Thomas Photos; Ross Tse; Scott Brandt; Charles Sullivan, **Cambridge Historical Commission;** William Cornelia; S. Scott Hutchinson; Richard Lucas; Mitch Frumkin; Ilene Shaw, Gary Rovenska and Adrienne Ross, **J.C. Whitney/Warshawsky;** Jay Peck; Phil Toy; Hub Willson; Tony Eboli; Tim Kerwin; Phillips Camera House; Michael Brown; Frank Lipo, **Historical Society of Oak Park and River Forest, IL;** Mike Moya; Gene's Studio; Al Ferreira; David Jensen; Lou Puckelis, **Chicago Motor Club; University of Akron Archives;** Mike McKernan, **Superior Coaches;** Steve Tracey, **P&S Group;** Tom McPherson, **Specialty Vehicle Press;** Barbara Dunn, **Hawaiian Historical Society;** Charlene Noyes, Harry Sweet, and Nikki Pahl, **Sacramento Archives and Museum Collection Center;** Dr. John W. Little; Joe Rodrigus, **Hanna Sherman, International;** Kim Bartley, **White Castle System, Inc.**

**OWNERS**
Special thanks to the owners of the cars featured in this book for their enthusiastic cooperation.

**1950:** Paul A. Leinbohm; Dr. Tom Eganhouse; Edward Giacobrazzi; Danny L. Steine; Loren E. Miller; Frank C. Guzzo; Dan and Barb Baltic; Roy E. Schneckloth; Wayne Laska; John Pollack; Paul and Peg Mather; Dix Helland; Ray Tomb; Clarence Becker; Joseph C. Ezell; Larry K. Landis; Roy Yost; Robert G. Seals; Donald L. Muchmore; Philomena Ronco Kohan; Arthur J. Sabin; Robert Heimstra.

**1951:** Tom Andrews; Jeff Walther/Jeff Walther Dodge; Rich and Norma Felschow; David Doyle; Donald W. Peters; Dells Auto Museum; Jim Stewart; Anthony J. Gullatta; Cal and Nancy L. Beauregard; Bob Ward; Earl Heintz; Edward George Allen; Earl J. Carpenter; Bill Goodsene; Bill Burgun; Bonnie and Dennis Statz; William D. Albright; Doug Burnell; William Tresize; Brook Stevens; John Keck; Chuck and Charlotte Watson; Keith Zimmerman; Jack Mueller; Victor Jacoellis; Gary McClaine; Steve Carey; Henry Smith; Jerry Jaragosky; Bonnie Carey; Henry Smith; Chuck Rizzo; Ken Netwig; Greg Pagano; James L. Dowdy; Jack Karleskind; James C. Pardo; Bobby Wiggins; Robert Rocchio; Bob Hassinger; William G. Burgun; Doug Burnell; Rosemary and Duane Sell; Steve Carey; Hudson D. Firestone; Henry Smith; Verne Leyendecker/Classical Gas; George S. Jewell.

**1952:** Robert Frumkin; Keith Cullen; Jerry Tranberger; John L. Murray; Alvin Buechele; Charles O. Sharpe; Bob Adams Collectibles, Ltd.; Jerry Ferguson; John R. Vorval; Richard Clements; John Sanders; Bill Burgun; Harrah National Auto Museum; Jerry Johnson; Lowell Johnson; Brooks Stevens Museum; George A. Buchinger; Phil and Louella Crus; Alan and Wilma Jordan; Steve Megyes; Lewis E. Retzer; Douglas J. Smith; Tom Mcdowell; George Pitts; Glen and Vera Reints; Edward J. Ostrowski; John J. and Minnie G. Keys; Chuck Bernecker; Bob and Brad Chandler; Homer Jay Sanders, Sr.; Robert Gernhofer; Bill Burgun; Bobby Wiggins; Carl and Mary Allen; Henry Patrick; Jerry Johnson.

**1953:** Bob Brannon; Bill Knudsen and John White; Briggs Cunningham Museum; Tim Graves; Stanley and Phyllis Dumes; Mitchell Corporation of Owosso; H.H. Wheeler, Jr.; William R. Lindsey; Kurt Fredricks; Gary Gettleman; F. James Garbe; Carl Noll; Norman Plogge; Dr. Ernie Hendry; John Rikert; Dorothy Clemmer; Hank Roeters; Dale and Marily Dutoni; Paul and Nancy Vlcek Jr.; Dick Choler; Bortz Auto Collection; William D. Albright; Bob Hill; Jerry Johnson; John E. Parker; Dale Osten; James Saicheck; Gerald Newton; Steve LeFevre; J. Saicheck; Dr. Douglas L. Bruinsma; Richard Presson; Deer Park Car Museum; Wayne R. Graefen; Bob and Wendi Walker.

**1954:** Frederick J. Roth; David Emery; Frank and Gene Sitarz; Everett Michaels; Robert Hetzel; Forrest D. Howell; Richard and Janice Plastino; Ray Ostrander; Suburban Motors, Tucson, Arizona; Ed Oberhaus; Erville Murphy; Eugene Vaughn; Thomas Armstrong; Thomas H. Peterson; Robert Babcock; Bill and Dorothy Harris; James and John Sharp; Virgil and Dorothy Meyer; Dwight Cervin; Cal and Lori Middleton; Bob Shapiro; Joe Bortz; James A. Milemak; Roger Clements; George Lucie; Jim Mueller; Ted Freeman; Norman Kirchner; Roy Umberger; Norman W. Prien; Bob Webber; Robert C. Fox; Rachel Markos; David L. Stanilla; Howard Johnson; Fritz Hugo; Jim Clark.

**1955:** Tom Griffith; Warren P. Lubich; George P. Valiukas; Gary Richards; Ed Tolhurst; Gary L. Walker; Greg Gustafson; Kennedith Turner; Charles M. Havelka; David L. Ferguson; Carl Herren; Nolan Adams; Bob and Frances Shaner; Vern Burkitt; Dennis Flint; Albie Albershardt; Bill Barbee; Richard Matson; William Lauer; R. McAtee; Jerry Avard; Myron Davis; Otto T. Rosenbush; Jeff and Aleta Wells; Lester Schnepen; Bob and Janet Nitz; Arthur and Suzanne Dalby; Harry Demenge; Leonard Quinlin; O'Ceola Sloan; Stuart Echols; Mervin Afflerbach; Bob Strous; Dan and Karen Bilyeu; Peter McNicholl; Alan C. Parker; Don and Sue Fennig; Tom Franks; Fred and Diane Ives; Warren P. Lubich; John Riordon; Bill and Lanee Proctor; Leroy Janisch; Mac Horst; Kennedith and Wayne Turner; Bill Groves; Joe Malta; Richard Kalinowski; Jim Cahill; Bill Curran; Gene R. Deblasio Jr.; Paul Eggerling; Ron Welch; Norb Kopchinski; Terry McElfresh; Jack Gratzianna; Clayton E. Bone; June Trombley; Tom Null; Kenneth G. Lindsey; Raymond and Marylin Benoy; Jim Wickel; Harold Gibson; Joseph R. Bua.

**1956:** Edmund L. Gibes; Ed Wassmann; Glendon and Betty Kierstead; Bob Adams; Burt Carlson; Robert W. Paige; Richard Brinker; A. La Rue Plotts, Jr.; B. Stevens and J. Wolfe; James C. Lipka; Roger and Connie Graeber; Jack E. Moore; Stan and Betty Hankins; Dick Rosynek; Kathy Barber; Dick Roynek; Bill Stone; Paul Hem; Art and Vicky Hoock; John and Peggy Clinton; Brian Long; Alan Wendland; Ray and Nancy Deitke; Edward R. Keshen; Dennis Hauke; M. Randall Mytar; David Barry; David Senholz; Edwin C. Kirstatter; Mary Jaeger; John V. Cavanugh; Michael Vacik; Allen Spethman; Orville Dopps; James R. Cunningham; Ron Pittman; Gary Johns; Sherry Echols; Eugene Sinda, Jr.; Jeff Dranson; Edward S. Kuziel; Dave Higby; Charles and Veronica Wurm, Jr.; Kenneth Regnier; Jim Bombard; Robert J. Matteoli; Charlene H. Arora; John Krempasky; Dr. Art Burrichter; Henry T. Heinz; Steve Williams; Jerry Kill; Dave Hill; Jay Harrigan; Chicago Car Exchange; Studebaker National Museum; Bob Peiler; David Hill; Lester H. Hooley; Donald L. Waite; Donald G. Elder; Robert Sexton; Ken Carmack; Jim Scarpitti; Wayne Davis Restoration; Hank Kubicki; Don Simpkin; William B. Edwards; Robb Petty; Don Wendel; Ross Gibaldi; Paul A. Buscemi; Russell and Shirley Dawson; Michael Vacik; Eli Lader; Sheldon Grover; Kenneth Geiger; Joseph Minnetto; Edward Ballenger II; Kenneth Ugolini; Robert Sexton.

**1957:** Monte McElroy; Frank R. Magyar; Eldon Anson; Robb Petty; Charles G. Roveran; Paul F. Northam; William R. Lindsey; James and Susan Verhasselt; Bob Rose; David and Ann Kurtz; Tom and Karen Barnes; Joe Bortz; Alan C. Hoff; Frank R. Bobek; Richard Zeiger, MD; Wayne Rife; Noel Blanc; Bill Ulrich; Larry Hill; Dennis McNamara; Dave Higby; Bernie and Ann Buller; Glenn R. Bappe; David L. Goetz; Dennis M. Statz; John Krempasky; Dick Hoyt; Michael Wehling; Tim and Sharon Hacker; Bernard Powell; Herbert Wehling; Donald R. Lawson; Harry E. Downing; Neil S. Black; Bob Aaron; Bud Hiler; Dr. William H. Lenharth; Terry Davies; Dale and Roxanne Carrington; Richard E. Bilter; David L. Griebling; Ken Block; Richard Carpenter; Jim D. Gregorio; Jess Ruffalo; Tom Devers; John and Susan Gray; Charles Phoenix; David Rosenfield; Vito S. Ranks; Bill Warren; Neil Vetter; John J. Oakes, Jr.; Ralph M. Hartsock; Jess Ruffalo; David Lawrence; Tom Devers; Sherwood Kahlenberg; Bob Schmidt; Ross Gibaldi; Amos Minter; Jerry Capizzi; J.W. Silveira; Fraser Dante Limited; Jim Ferrero; Julie M. Braritz; Denis Beauregard; George Swartz; Gordon Christl; John W. Petras/Classic Chrome; Brian L. Kelly; Jerry L. Keller; Glyn and Jan Rawley.

**1958:** Dean Ullman; George Berg; S. Holloran; J. Alexander; Maurice B. Hawa; Vern Hunt; Jack Sawyer; William Amos; Charles Hilbert; Art Gravatt; Dr. Gerrard DePersio; John P. Fitzgerald; John Scopelite; Jerry Cinotti; Barry and Barb Bales; Mario Gutierrez; Jim DiGregorio; Richard Daly; Thomas L. Karkiewicz; Bob Mongomery; Gary Mills; Wayne Essary; Marvin Wallace; Andrew Alphonso; Michael J. Morelli; Gene Povinelli; Neil W. Sugg; Christopher Antal; Jeff Ruffalo; Jim Crossen; Tim Fagan; Bob and Brad Chandler; Jim Mueller; Virgil Hudkins; Andrew Krizwan; Joel Twainten; Aaron Kahlenberg; Christopher Antal; Dennis L. Huff; Ted Maupin; Jerry Capizzi; Michael L. Berzenye; Ruth Dulik; Robert P. Hallada; Bruce Sansone; John Sobers; Michael D. McCloskey; Dean Ullman; Buddy Pepp; Darryl Salisbury; Douglas Suter; Frank Wrenick.

**1959:** T.L. Ary; Ted Hinkle; Bob and Roni Sue Shapiro; Dennis B. Miracky; Mervin M. Afflerbach; Bill Lauer; Richard Carpenter c/o Yesterday Once More; Jon Hardy; Bill Henefelt; Robert and Diane Adams; Wendi Walker; Charles A. Rublaitus; David Frieday; Dr. John W. Little; Dennis Huff; Edsel Ford; William R. Kipp; Steve and Dawn Cizmas; Classic Car Center; Eric Hopman; Walter J. Smith; Don R. Kreider; Harrah National Auto Museum; Glen and Fay Erb; Elmer and Shirley Hungate; J. Franklin; S. Halloran; Harold Stabe; Ray Geschke; Orville Dopps; Christine and Robert Waldock; Bob Moore; Bill Schweitz; Joe Wenzlich; Al Schaefer; Bill Stearns; Barry and Barb Bales; Don and Bonnie Snipes.

# Table of Contents

As the decade begins, automakers are still striving to meet the pent-up demand for cars that was created when the industry shut down during World War II. Studebaker debuts new "bullet-nose" models, and nearly all manufacturers prosper—but not for long.

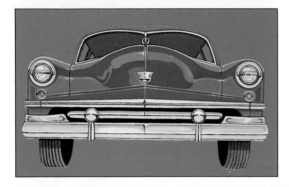

Independents Kaiser and Packard offer new designs, but most manufacturers serve up only facelifts. That's all that is needed: With the war in Korea looming, buyers fearing another shut-down keep demand high.

Ford, Lincoln, and Mercury all boast new styling, but their industry rankings don't improve. Despite production cutbacks by almost all automakers in the face of the Korean War, sales begin to slump, and cars start to pile up on dealers' lots.

Highlights include Chevrolet's legendary Corvette, a trio of "custom" GM ragtops, and Studebaker's classic "Loewy" coupes, but a turnaround in the seller's market causes Ford and Chevy to duke it out in a sales blitz—to the detriment of the independents.

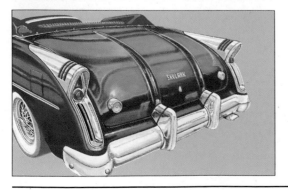

Buick and Cadillac tone down their specialty convertibles (Olds drops its version), and the public tones down its desire for Detroit's wares. In a slow-down year for the industry, Ford beats Chevrolet in the production race for the first time since '49.

A great year for the Big Three turns into a dismal year for the independents. Chrysler Corporation and GM bring out exciting new designs wrapped around powerful V-8 engines, while the independents wither—and some die.

Despite modern styling and brilliant engineering, the proud Packard nameplate graces its last luxury automobile. After record-shattering '55 sales, the industry generally coasts on the styling front, but engines get bigger and brawnier.

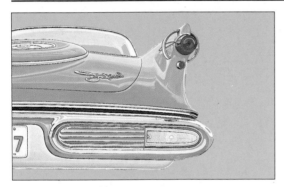

No doubt about it, the horsepower race is in full swing, and tailfins reach new heights—particularly at Chrysler Corporation, which advances its "Forward Look." Sales rebound, but the industry faces some dark days ahead.

Detroit unleashes bigger, flashier cars—just as the economy unleashes a recession. This spells trouble for most mid-priced makes, but spells *disaster* for Ford's new entry. It isn't just the "horse-collar" grille that dooms the Edsel....

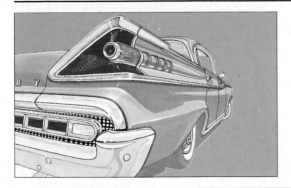

In deference to a sudden interest in economy, compacts rise in popularity and the horsepower race momentarily slows to a near standstill. But tailfins gain in prominence, even on normally conservative Ford Motor Company products.

# Foreword

Looking back, the Fifties are remembered as a decade of vitality, of prosperity, of unabashed promise. Americans saw the economy zooming, babies booming—and the Cold War looming.

In our collective memories, at least, it was a time of innocence: of simple pleasures and basic values, linked with boundless enthusiasm. This was also a decade of conformity, as families scurried for security. But more than most Americans realized, these were also years of profound change. Television overtook radio as the foremost influence on popular culture. Rock 'n' roll, unheard of as the decade opened, developed into a major force. McDonald's made the scene.

Labor-saving devices filled the ranch-style homes of the growing suburbs. The Depression mentality finally was fading, elbowed aside by a "buy now, pay later" philosophy. Jobs were plentiful—until a recessionary downturn in 1958 took millions of upward-strivers by surprise.

In the friendlier Fifties, even the celebrity scandals were mild. Politicians weren't yet reviled. And the local filling station was staffed by attendants eager to wash your windshield, check your oil, fill your tank *and* your tires, and oftentimes award you a "free gift with every fill-up."

Looking deeper, we find that the decade wasn't quite so simple as people like to believe. *Ozzie and Harriet* might have served as role models for America, but not all citizens led TV-style lives. Teens were just as confused and misunderstood as in later years. Back-seat romances flourished, if unacknowledged by parents—though any suitor arriving in a Nash, with its famous "mobile motel" fold-down seats, was sure to get the cold shoulder from his date's father. Respect for authority reigned, but stirrings of rebellion began to emerge.

For those smitten with the automotive fever, though, this was a singularly glorious epoch. Only Detroit had the cure, and its prescription was doled out every fall to great fanfare.

TV sets broadcast the latest shapes, radios blared the car companies' catchy jingles. Young car buffs scanned magazine pages for pictures of the spanking-new mechanical attractions. Errands demanded an end run past dealers' row, just to see if the paper coverings had yet been torn down from the showroom windows to reveal the splendor of next year's models.

6

As the Fifties began, 40 million automobiles roamed American roads. Three out of five families owned one. Automakers still were trying to satiate pent-up demand for new cars. Several independent makes had sprouted, notably Kaiser and Frazer. Others had been around since before World War II: Crosley, Hudson, Nash, Packard, Studebaker, Willys. Imports trickled into American ports.

As manufacturers met—then exceeded—the nation's automotive appetite, sales began to sag. Ford and Chevrolet waged a price war in 1953 that injured the independents far more than the "Big Three" (General Motors, Ford Motor Company, and Chrysler Corporation).

Crosley, discovering that Americans weren't yet ready for subcompacts, dropped out after 1952. Kaiser sighed its last gasp in '55. Hudson and Packard soon followed. Nash diminished to its compact Rambler spinoff. Studebaker gained a temporary reprieve only by virtue of its well-timed '59 Lark compact.

Meanwhile, the horsepower race that had begun with the Rocket Oldsmobiles in '49, then escalated to Chrysler "Hemis" and Chevrolet V-8s, progressed into a leapfrogging bout. Cars, too, grew bigger—and presumably better, in a culture that tended to equate the two. Chrome oozed from every panel. Tailfins, having started small, sprouted beyond belief. The Edsel quickly came and went: a noble hope for 1958, a synonym for failure by '60.

Styling took over from engineering as the driving force behind sales. Automatic transmissions began to edge aside traditional stickshifts. Power gadgetry blossomed, climaxing with Ford's elaborate retractable hardtops.

Pillarless four-doors joined their two-door mates. Three-tone paint jobs appeared. Station wagons emerged as the vehicle of choice in growing suburbia.

This book presents it all. While automobiles serve as its hub, *Cars of the '50s* is more than a mere "car book." Instead, it's a spirited romp through a period that's filled with fond memories for those who lived it, and inspires awe—and often disbelief—in the generations that came after.

American cars exemplified the spirit of those times: brawny and proud, hopeful and boastful, strong and special. We hope you find this tribute to the '50s as colorful and stirring as the decade itself.

# 1950

America was changing rapidly as the 1950s began—and the pace was about to pick up. World War II had been over for half a decade. Memories of the Great Depression grew blurred. Families began their migration to the suburbs, which sprouted like tentacles around the nation's cities.

Kids watched Howdy Doody on 12-inch black-and-white TV sets, and spent Saturdays at 15-cartoon matinees. Rock 'n' roll hadn't yet been heard—though an occasional burst of jazz or rhythm and blues might jar the air. Sex was a private matter, violence rare. People knew their neighbors.

Veterans and civilians who'd endured privation in the past now faced a cornucopia of consumer goods—and were determined to enjoy the bounty. Women who'd toiled in factories and offices during the war resumed their roles as housewives, making

8

Dad—more often than not—the sole breadwinner. Even with a single salary, though, most folks had money to spend.

Incomes had risen steadily, despite a wave of strikes. Median family income topped $3300 a year. Manufacturing workers earned an average $56.20 per week—a new high. A loaf of bread cost 14 cents, pork chops ran 75 cents a pound, and a half-gallon of milk sold for 41 cents—delivered to your door.

Not every sign was positive. Unemployment hit 7 percent in January—up from 4.5 percent a year earlier, setting a postwar record. Still, the American Dream was simple enough: a good job, well-behaved family, pleasant home. Oh, and one more thing—an impressive automobile.

In the hardest of times, Americans of modest means had struggled to maintain an automobile, even if it was a jalopy. Now, men who'd once taken a streetcar to their jobs not only wanted, but *needed* a reliable car. Before long, their wives and children would be wanting one of their own.

By 1950, some 39.6 million passenger cars traveled American roads—40-percent more than in 1941. Three fifths of American families owned one, but the average car was 7.8 years old.

When World War II ended, automakers had nothing fresh to offer car-hungry Americans; they simply issued mildly revised prewar models. Studebaker was first with a completely new design, which debuted for 1947. By then, Henry Kaiser and Joe Frazer had joined forces, producing cars under both names. A year later, Hudson launched its low-slung "Step-down" design, and the new Cadillac body displayed the first tailfins.

Most automakers waited until 1949 to release redesigned models. Meanwhile, some new manufacturers tried their hand. Best known is the Tucker, of which 51 were built before legal troubles ended its day in the limelight. There was also a Davis three-wheeler, a Bobbi-Kar—even a couple of flying cars.

Chevrolet and Pontiac launched curvy new bodies for 1949. Ford chose a boxier (but tasteful) shape, while companions Lincoln and Mercury showed more roundness. Chrysler products stood steadfastly upright. Nash went wild, with an aerodynamic form that many said resembled an "upside-down bathtub."

One new body style emerged, this from GM. Called the "hardtop convertible," it melded the vitality of a convertible with the practicality of a closed coupe.

Through the late '40s, demand was stronger than automakers could hope to fulfill. By 1950, though, nearly all designs were at least a year old, and the seller's market was subsiding. Manufacturers had to deliver something fresh, something exciting, if they hoped to continue the strong sales totals.

But not yet. With only a few exceptions, facelifts were the order of the year. Most 1950 models—Chevrolet and Plymouth to Hudson and Nash—showed little more than touch-ups. Studebaker's innovative "bullet nose," for instance, led a body that differed little from its 1947-49 predecessor.

Several more automakers introduced automatic transmissions. Available in Oldsmobiles since 1940, automatics took their time in gaining converts. Chrysler products and Hudsons had *semi*-automatics, which retained a clutch but changed gears as the driver's foot let up on the gas pedal.

One-piece curved windshields appeared on more makes, such as Cadillac and Oldsmobile, joining those from '49 or before. Buick announced low-glare glass.

Because truth in advertising was not yet an issue, automakers could claim their products were the handsomest, the most frugal—or simply the best, period. Pontiac, for instance, declared its dashboard "the most beautiful in the industry." Hudson called its cars "safest" (not without validity, in view of their rigid construction).

Without quite realizing it, Oldsmobile managed to set off a "horsepower race" that would overtake the industry. All the engineers did was create a short-stroke, overhead-valve V-8: the '49 Rocket engine. Far more efficient than inline and L-head engines that powered most cars, the ohv V-8 would become the engine of choice for a new breed of driver—the hot rodder—and for millions of ordinary Americans.

Chevrolet and Ford had pondered a *small* American car, but only Powel Crosley enjoyed some triumph in that realm. After a strong 1948, however, Crosley's star began to fade, reaching the sick list by 1950. Americans liked *big* cars—a craving destined to flourish. Yet Nash took another tack, launching the first successful compact: Rambler.

Quite a few automakers cut prices on 1950 models. As a result, a whopping 6,663,461 cars (8,004,242 total vehicles) were built—an all-time record, 30 percent above the '49 total. Meanwhile, the Federal Reserve Board placed stricter limits on credit—an issue destined to rise again as incomes trailed the public's urge for automobiles.

Americans finally were managing to forget war. Then, on June 25, President Truman ordered U.S. troops to Korea in a "police action" that would last for several years. Fear of wartime shortages triggered a car-buying frenzy. In December, a "state of emergency" was proclaimed.

Auto production never halted, as it had during World War II, but certain raw materials wound up in short supply, and makers faced output limits. No matter. As 150 million Americans thirsted for private transport, Detroit was eager to provide.

# Chrysler Corporation

Chrysler products earn mild facelift of "box-on-box" shape

Company marks 25th anniversary

Longer rear fenders hold flush-mounted taillights, and back windows grow in size . . . flat two-piece windshields remain

Hardtop coupes arrive late in model year, from Chrysler, DeSoto, and Dodge

Chrysler's posh Imperial and Town & Country hardtop adopt four-wheel disc brakes

Ignition-key starter switches replace former pushbuttons

Chryslers carry six-cylinder or straight-eight engines; DeSoto, Dodge, and Plymouth have sixes only

Chrysler, DeSoto, and Dodge use semi-automatic transmissions; Plymouth sticks with plain three-speed column shift

Final "woody" station wagons go on sale

Strike begins January 25, lasts 14½ weeks—yet record 1.27 million cars are built

DeSoto's output jumps 42 percent, but market share sinks

Plymouth builds 610,954 cars, yet dips to fourth— behind Buick

Long-time president K.T. Keller is named chairman . . . "Tex" Colbert takes the presidency

1. Chrysler immodestly declared its "distinguished" New Yorker and Saratoga the "finest in the fine car field." Their 135-bhp Spitfire straight eight had "the speed of the wind." 2. Formerly a wood-structure convertible, the Town & Country became a Newport hardtop, with white-ash framing attached to steel body panels. Just 700 were built, this year only. 3. Cars wearing a Chrysler badge included the eight-cylinder New Yorker, Saratoga, T&C, and Imperial, plus Royal and Windsor sixes. 4. Leather topped foam rubber on the Safety-Cushion dashboard. At 13 mph or more, Prestomatic slipped into high gear as the driver let up on the gas.

The *Beautiful* 1950 **CHRYSLER** *Town & Country* NEWPORT

*Now . . . Now . . . New in every detail that says: "Thoroughbred"*

TODAY'S NEW STYLE CLASSIC . . .

❝The public likes a car that is designed primarily to ride in, with its appearance governed by its functions.❞

*Chrysler Division general sales manager* **Joseph A. O'Malley***; January 1950*

**1.** Far cheaper than an eight, the six-cylinder Windsor promised "breathtaking beauty." **2.** A Newport hardtop mixed a convertible's "low-swept road-hugging lines" with steel-roofed protection. Clearbac rear windows used three sections of curved glass. **3.** In addition to summer fun, a Windsor convertible promised to be "the sweetest running car in America." **4.** Back when service stations made house calls, the "chaser" motorcycle was towed behind the customer's car, here a Chrysler Highlander. **5.** Except up front, can you tell that this stripped "movie car" is a New Yorker? **6.** Station wagons came only in the Royal series, with an all-steel or "woody" body. **7.** With rear seat folded, a wagon's loading platform measured nearly 10 feet long.

# 1950 DeSoto

**1.** All DeSotos had 112-horsepower six-cylinder engines, including this $2174 Custom four-door sedan, pictured in the sales brochure. The make had been named for Spanish explorer Hernando de Soto. In addition to regular and eight-passenger sedans, DeSoto's Custom line included a wagon, hardtop coupe, club coupe, and convertible, but the sedan accounted for nearly two-thirds of production.
**2.** Interiors of a Custom DeSoto sedan were better appointed than those of the more utilitarian DeLuxe series. DeSoto promoted its cars' plentiful "hat room," as well as "big, wide doors [that] let you walk in . . . not wiggle in!" **3.** Dashboards were recessed to allow more leg room, and the ignition key operated the starter switch. Instrument faces displayed a new metallic gold sheen. Tip-Toe hydraulic shift and Fluid Drive, standard on the Custom series, required use of the clutch only to shift into Reverse or Low gear. **4.** Easy-to-operate radio and heater controls were placed "within instant reach." **5.** Most Custom (shown) and DeLuxe DeSotos rode a 125.5-inch wheelbase. Minor styling revisions included a wider grille and new flush-mounted taillights that included the stoplight; formerly, DeSotos had a separate center-mounted stoplight.

1. DeSoto's DeLuxe series comprised a four-door sedan (shown), club coupe, eight-passenger sedan, and Carry-All sedan. Chrome was abundant—and would increase through the decade. 2. Just 969 DeSoto eight-passenger sedans were produced, mainly in the Custom series, on a stretched (139.5-inch) wheelbase. Most served as limousines or in commercial fleets. 3. With the top down on a summer's day, a Custom convertible coupe delighted the senses. Only 2900 were built, with a $2578 price tag. 4. Customers who liked the look of a convertible but appreciated the comforts of an all-steel top could now choose a Sportsman hardtop. Part of the Custom series, it cost $89 less than a true ragtop, but sold better—despite a debut very late in the model year. Fender skirts were popular accessories in the early Fifties. 5. A DeSoto Suburban seated nine, plus a supply of luggage—augmented by the roof rack. At $3179, it was the most costly DeSoto. 6. Most of this year's 700 DeSoto station wagons wore wood, but only the all-steel version would carry on. 7. The 112-bhp, 236.6-cid Powermaster L-head six promised "flashing performance, faster getaway." 8. Chair-height seats gave DeLuxe sedan occupants lots of headroom.

# 1950 Dodge

1

2

**1.** Despite a shorter (115-inch) wheelbase than other models, a Wayfarer sedan also seated six. Dodge aimed the "nimble" semi-fastback—priced just above the most costly Plymouths—at "value-conscious" buyers. **2.** A foursome wouldn't fit inside a Wayfarer Sportabout roadster, but it could probably carry all their clubs. Some dealers added a small rear seat to augment the three-passenger front bench. **3.** Roll-up windows and vent wings could be added "at slight extra cost" to the Sportabout's $1727 base price. A mere 2903 were built. **4-5.** Penny-pinchers could get a Wayfarer three-passenger coupe for just $1611, featuring a huge trunk, plus storage behind the single seat. **6.** Dodge's new Coronet Diplomat hardtop cost $96 less than a convertible. **7.** The rear seat in a Coronet station wagon folded forward, making a space nearly eight feet long. **8.** Like Chrysler and DeSoto, Dodge had a long-wheelbase sedan with two folding seats.

3

4

6

5

7

8

> "Dodge's production and retail deliveries this year have been the highest in Dodge history. We are confident that we will do even better with our new, improved automobiles."

*Dodge president* **L L "Tex" Colbert**, *on the plus points of the 1950 Dodge line; December 1949*

1. Like all Chrysler products, Dodge got a facelift. A Meadowbrook four-door sedan cost $79 less than a Coronet, but had the same wheelbase and 103-bhp Get-Away L-head engine. 2. Roomy interiors allowed occupants to sit up straight "without any danger of knocking your hat off," in extra-wide seats. 3. A restyled dashboard held three square dials and matching accessories. 4. "Your toe does it all," Dodge claimed of its new Gyro-Matic transmission. Available only on Coronets, it had a "sprint-away" passing gear and a "power range" for steep grades. 5. A person could enter and leave a Coronet sedan "without twisting or squirming." Because the rear footrest was fixed, leg room wasn't affected by the position of the driver's seat.

## packed with value and ready to prove it!

Here's the sensational new standard for excellence in the low-priced car field — the brilliant new, value-packed Plymouth!

No other car at the price gives you anything like the new Plymouth's great engineering advantages. The speed and ease of Ignition Key starting . . . the thrilling performance of the 7.0 to 1 high compression en-gine . . . the swift, smooth stops of big Safe-Guard Hydraulic Brakes . . . the positive blowout protection of Safety-Rim Wheels.

The new Plymouth rides like a heavy, high-priced limousine yet handles with amazing ease! No wonder this fine car of great value is now — more than ever — *the car that likes to be compared!* No wonder this new American Beauty is now — more than ever — *the low-priced car most like high-priced cars!*

Plan to visit your nearby Plymouth dealer now. He'll gladly arrange for a demonstration drive. Then you can test this car and see for yourself that the new Plymouth is the most car value you can possibly buy at Plymouth's low price!

 **NOW** — *more than ever — the car that likes to be compared*

PLYMOUTH Division of CHRYSLER CORPORATION, Detroit 31, Michigan

1

1. Ads accurately pushed value and engineering, but Plymouth's 97-horsepower engine didn't quite deliver the promised "thrilling performance." Solid and reliable they were, but few folks outside Chrysler Corp. deemed Plymouths stylish. 2. A bright Special DeLuxe convertible looked quite jaunty, despite its boxy profile. Copywriters concocted names for just about every technical feature, so Plymouths had such items as Safe-Guard brakes and Safety-Rim wheels. 3. Only the wagon cost more than a Plymouth convertible, which featured pleated upholstery. 4. Ice-cold root beer cost a nickel at this A&W stand in Alton, Illinois. Drive-ins and carhops already were busy, but the fast-food craze wouldn't take hold for a few more years.

2

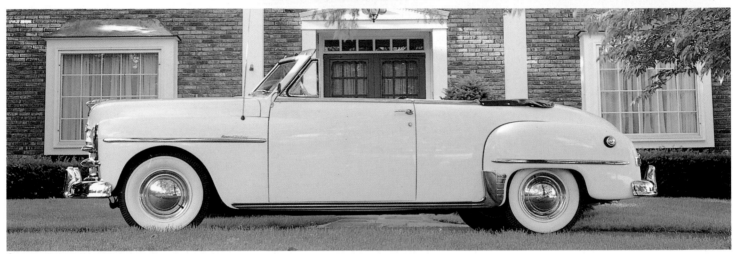

3

4

# Crosley Motors, Inc.

Just $882 buys a Crosley sedan, while Chevrolets start at $1329 . . . average full-time workers earn $2992 yearly

Super Sports roadster debuts, joining similarly low-slung Hotshot

Full line also includes sedan, station wagon, convertible

FarmORoad debuts in July—serves as car, truck, light tractor

Crosley's 44-cid engine develops 26.5 bhp

Drum brakes return at midyear, after brief flirtation with trouble-prone discs

Sales begin to sag after some success with enlarged postwar model

Only 6792 Crosleys are produced, including 742 roadsters—far below the 28,734 units issued in 1948

Price cuts in June fail to jump-start sales totals

As earnings rise and suburbs grow, Americans crave *big* automobiles, shunning this pioneering subcompact

Passenger cars are criticized for quirky handling and top-heavy shape

Crosley announces Quicksilver engine—runs on gasoline plus water-alcohol injection

Lesser-known minicars include Brogan, Imp, King Midget, Playboy

**1**

1. Crosley's Hotshot, introduced for 1949, was a genuine sports car. A mildly modified engine could push the Spartan, bug-eyed roadster to 77 mph—or even 90, if fitted with aftermarket hop-up gear. Scaled-down doors were optional. **2.** Just two people fit in the down-to-basics interior of a Hotshot. Note the add-on turn-signal unit. **3.** For 1950, a better-trimmed Super Sports convertible—complete with doors—joined the no-frills Hotshot. Both had a deck-mounted spare tire. Small, thrifty, inexpensive to buy and build, Crosley sedans and sportsters were two decades ahead of their time.

**2**

**3**

**4**

4. Crosley's tiny $795 FarmORoad served as a car, truck, tractor—or even a portable power source. Note the dual rear wheels. A back seat could be added.

# Ford Motor Company

Ford, Lincoln, and Mercury get facelifts after radical '49 restyling

Ford brand slips to second place in volume, with production of 1.2 million cars—nearly 290,000 behind Chevrolet

Market share hits 24 percent—highest since 1930s

New Ford crest decorates hood and trunk lid

Pushbutton door handles replace pull units; gas filler hides beneath fender flap

Fords come with six-cylinder or V-8 engine; Mercury and Lincoln are V-8 only

Ford launches padded-roof Crestliner sports sedan . . . Lincoln Lido and Capri, and Mercury Monterey also wear padded tops

Lincolns may be ordered with Hydra-Matic, bought from GM

New York Fashion Academy names Ford "Fashion Car" for second year in a row

Lincolns again feature recessed headlights

Mercury adds short-lived Thrifty series

A Mercury wins its class in the Mobilgas Economy Run . . . another paces the Indianapolis 500 race

A Lincoln finishes ninth in the first Mexican Road Race

Ads insist V-8 engine "whispers while it works"

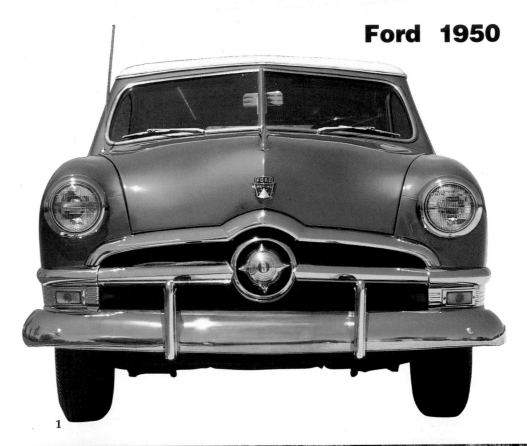

1

2

1. An "8" within a Ford grille "spinner" revealed the presence of the fabled flathead V-8 engine. A new hood crest, based on a 17th-century coat of arms, replaced 1949's block lettering. Taller and wider than arch-rival Chevrolet, Fords came in DeLuxe or Custom trim, with six-cylinder or V-8 power. 2. Lacking a hardtop coupe like Chevy's, Ford launched a sporty Crestliner Tudor sedan with a padded vinyl roof. Ribbed fender skirts accented its sleek look. Priced $200 above a plain Custom Tudor, Crestliners came in three vivid two-tone blends, including Sportsman Green and black. 3. Here, one of the year's 50,299 convertibles gets a fill-up with premium—and full-service attention—at a Sunoco station.

3

# 1950 Ford

**1.** Spotting twin Fords at a stoplight wasn't uncommon, as evidenced by this '50 scene in Moline, Illinois. Note the 25-cent parking-lot charge. **2.** Ford wagons went to 22,929 customers, and would eventually become hot items on the used-car market. Laminated maple framing was attached to the wagon's steel body panels. **3.** A DeLuxe Tudor cost $1424; the business coupe, cheaper yet. **4.** Billed as "50 Ways New . . . 50 Ways Finer," Fords were much improved over '49. Bodies and frames were strengthened, handling improved, the V-8 engine quieted.

> **"** By taking advantage of the latest development in engine design we also have still further increased oil economy and added to the life of these engines. They are the quietest and smoothest-running engines we have ever produced. **"**
>
> *Ford engineering vice president* **Harold T. Youngren**, *on improvements to Ford's inline sixes and V-8s for model-year 1950; November 1949*

**5.** Introduced in 1932, Ford's L-head V-8 engine now displaced 239.4 cid and delivered 100 horsepower. Even in stock tune the V-8 had a strong performance edge over Chevrolet and Plymouth sixes. Note separate radiator hoses for each cylinder bank. **6.** Good Humor men took their jobs seriously, as evidenced by the almost military stance of these uniformed drivers. This popular fleet was made up of F-1 Ford trucks.

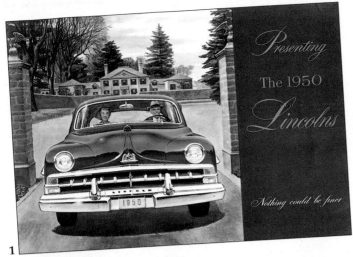

1. Judging by the dreary sales totals, not everyone agreed that "Nothing could be finer." Except for sunken headlights, Lincolns resembled an overweight Mercury. 2. A roomy Cosmopolitan coupe cost $3187 and rode a wheelbase four inches longer than regular Lincolns. The smaller models used Mercury body panels from the cowl back. 3. Long split rear-quarter windows on a Cosmopolitan coupe made it look more like a four-door. 4. No other car on the market had headlights like Lincoln's, but the idea failed to catch on. 5. As these lavish surroundings suggest, the fashion leader of the Lincoln line was the $3950 convertible, but only 536 went to customers. 6. Lowest-priced model, at $2529, was the basic six-passenger coupe.

**1.** Fender skirts helped enhance the Cosmopolitan coupe's profile, but the bulbous "bathtub" shape couldn't attract customers. Lincolns were luxurious, and rode beautifully. **2.** A Cosmopolitan sedan went for $3240. Note the three-piece rear window—a forerunner of soon-to-arrive wrap-around glass. Both models contained a 336.7-cid L-head V-8, rated at 152 bhp. **3-5.** Practically every American must have seen a photo of this stretched Cosmopolitan convertible sedan with retractable running boards, built for President Truman but used by the White House until 1961. Bodywork was by Raymond H. Dietrich, Inc. A decade later, Lincoln would reintroduce the convertible sedan as a production model. Nine limos also were ordered, with bodies by Henney. All were leased to the government.

**1.** Mercury offered a Lincoln-like look at a lower price. The 255-cid V-8, with an Econ-O-Miser carburetor, delivered 110 horsepower—10 more than Ford's. Touch-O-Matic overdrive claimed to cut fuel costs by 20 percent. **2.** A Mercury Sport Sedan cost almost $500 more than a Custom Ford Fordor. Both seated six. **3.** A pillarless hardtop wasn't feasible, so Mercury issued the Monterey. This one has been lowered, and sports a load of factory extras. **4.** For $177 more than a plain coupe, the Monterey got a vinyl roof—or canvas for $166. **5.** Mercury's $2561 wagon seated eight. **6.** An upright spare helped make efficient use of the spacious trunk. **7.** New fiberglass soundproofing quieted "the soft purr of the strong, silent" engine. **8.** A new Merco-Therm system delivered fresh air in any season.

1

2

3

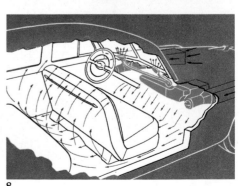

go for a ride and you'll go for **MERCURY**

4

5

6

7

8

23

# 1950 Mercury

1. "Smart, sleek-looking, massive," was Mercury's description of its $2412 convertible. 2. Families liked the Sport Sedan, making it the most popular model, but teens grew to favor the brash two-door. 3. Even in stock form, a fender-skirted club coupe looked rather dashing on the street. 4. Mercury's new Safe-T-Vue dash grouped gauges behind a single plexiglass panel. 5. Lounge Rest foam-rubber seats cradled a coupe's occupants.

6. In the new-car showroom, a smooth ride and smart stance tempted shoppers. Later, the "bathtub" Merc became an auto icon after film legend James Dean drove a '49 in *Rebel Without a Cause*. 7. A Mercury convertible, painted Mirada Yellow, paced the Indianapolis 500 race on May 30. 8. Driving the pace car was Lincoln-Mercury manager Benson Ford, with former racer and Speedway president Wilbur Shaw.

# General Motors Corporation

Corporation issues 3,653,358 U.S.-built vehicles

Pillarless hardtop coupes now available in all five GM makes

GM Motorama opens in New York; 350,000 visitors see show cars and production models

Buicks gain all-new body— so does Oldsmobile 98

Cadillac is in 48th year as "Standard of the World"

Cadillacs get new one-piece windshield, which also is phased in on Oldsmobiles

Second season for Cadillac's overhead-valve V-8 engine and Coupe de Ville body style

Chevrolets get optional Powerglide automatic

Oldsmobile issues final six-cylinder models

Rocket V-8 Oldsmobiles win 10 of 19 major stock-car races; Olds 88 sets class speed record at Daytona, reaching 100.28 mph

Pontiacs can have six- or eight-cylinder L-head engine—boast 28 styling/mechanical improvements

GM sales total a record $7.5 billion; net earnings amount to $834 million

Alfred Sloan, Jr., is GM chairman; Charles E. Wilson serves as president

1

66 This is the car of the future only in the sense that some of its design or mechanical features may appear some day in standard motorcars.

LeSabre is purely experimental. 99

*General Motors styling vice president **Harley J. Earl**, on the LeSabre show car; December 1950*

2

3

1. Super was the mid-level Buick, selling for $2139 as a four-door sedan. Buick's Special targeted low-budget buyers, while the Roadmaster was top-of-the-line. Dynaflow, Buick's automatic transmission, was standard in Roadmasters and optional in other Buicks. Available since 1948, the torque-converter unit soon earned such derisive nicknames as "Dyna-slush," mocking its smooth but slow takeoffs. 2. Harley J. Earl, head of GM's Art and Colour Section, earned credit for many styling touches, but few were more memorable than Cadillac's tailfins. By the late '50s, virtually all American cars—and even a few imports— would be sporting fins. 3. Buick Specials came in Tourback or fastback (sedanet) form. Note this four-door DeLuxe Tourback's three-piece rear window—a popular feature this year. 4. "Buick's the fashion for 1950," said the brochure. Roadmaster interiors ranked as "ultra-regal." All models adopted a single-unit bumper/grille.

4

# 1950 Oldsmobile

**1.** Only 2382 Oldsmobile 88 station wagons went to dealers. **2.** Launched a year earlier, the sharp 88 Holiday hardtop got some body/trim fine-tuning. Two-tones were popular. An 88 could accelerate to 60 mph in just over 12 seconds. Olds initially down-played performance, but it signaled the beginning of the horsepower race. **3.** Four-door sedans outsold all other body styles in all series; shown is a 76. **4.** At $1719, a club coupe was the cheapest 76. **5.** A pair of 88s stand ready to compete at Daytona Beach in 1950. **6.** Despite claims of "surging acceleration," the 105-bhp six paled in comparison to V-8 engines. **7.** Musical maestro Lawrence Welk poses with a full fleet of Olds 98s. **8.** British music-hall legend Gracie Fields looks pleased with this open 98. **9.** Olds promised not only swift pickup, but an "Air-Borne Ride." Coil springs soaked up the bumps at all four corners.

1

2

3

4

5

7

> **❝** Flying Saucers Amaze You? Our New Low Payments Are Even More Amazing. **❞**
>
> *Advertising slogan,*
> **House of Mozes** *used-car dealership, Philadelphia; May 1950*

6

8

9

1. Factory accessories added dash to a Pontiac Chieftain DeLuxe Eight sedan. Hydra-Matic and Vent-A-Shades added well-spent dollars to the $1908 base price. 2. Backup lights cost extra, as they did on most American cars. 3. Pontiacs carried their namesake's likeness on bright red badges. 4. Ads pushed value, as well as the spirited appearance of the new Catalina hardtop. 5. "America's lowest-priced straight-eight" engine grew in size and output, reaching 268.4 cid and 108 horsepower. 6. Sixes were powered by a 239.2-cid 90-bhp engine. 7. Except for wagons, a Chieftain DeLuxe convertible was the most costly Pontiac. 8. Fastbacks came only in the lower-cost Streamliner series. 9. Options on this Streamliner DeLuxe Eight include spotlights and a rear sunshade.

33

# 1950 Pontiac

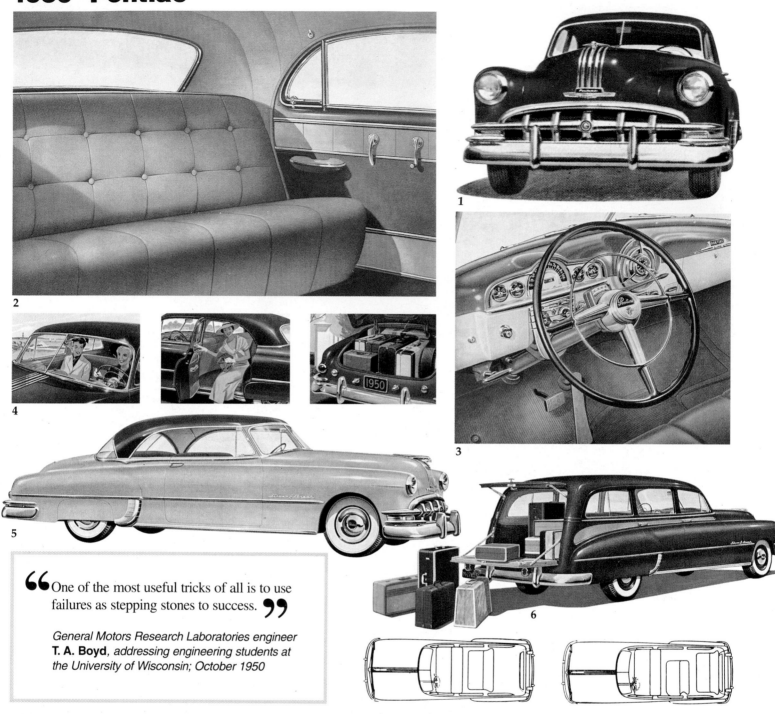

**66** One of the most useful tricks of all is to use failures as stepping stones to success. **99**

*General Motors Research Laboratories engineer* **T. A. Boyd,** *addressing engineering students at the University of Wisconsin; October 1950*

**1.** Pontiacs gained a bolder grille. The hood ornament could be plastic, lighting up as the headlights were switched on. **2.** "Everything a Fine Car should be" was Pontiac's claim for the interior decor. Rear seats were "restfully contoured." **3.** Dashboards were declared "the most beautiful in the industry," with a semicircular speedometer, round gauges, and a Handi-Grip parking brake. **4.** Styling touches included a "wide horizon windshield" with slim corner posts; wide, easy-access doors, with mating floor and sill "to avoid tripping and heel-catching"; and "Carry-More" trunk. **5.** A DeLuxe Catalina Eight hardtop cost $2069, but Pontiac also marketed a Super Catalina edition. Both were part of the Chieftain series. **6.** An all-steel Streamliner station wagon could hold six or eight passengers. **7.** Twin convertibles strutted proudly in a Chicago parade.

34

# Hudson Motor Car Company

Modest facelift helps give "Step-down" Hudsons a lower look

"Step-down" designation refers to the dropped floorpan, surrounded by frame girders

Hudsons are applauded for toughness and handling, as well as smooth highway ride

Shorter Pacemaker joins lineup—accounts for close to half of production

Pacemaker uses 232-cid six, rated 112 horsepower

Super Six engine boosted to 123 horsepower; aluminum cylinder head is available

Super and Commodore series can have either six- or eight-cylinder engine

Commodore outsells Super Six by two to one, despite its higher prices

Hudson offers three transmission options: mechanical overdrive, Drive-Master, and new Supermatic (which included a cruising gear)

Supermatic can be locked out, using dashboard button; shifts gears when letting up on gas

All Hudsons employ a Fluid-Cushioned clutch

Hudson ranks 13th in sales—worst showing since the war—on production of 121,408 cars

**1.** Owners of the "Step-down" Hudsons that arrived for 1948 cheered its low-slung design and easy-going ride. But because it was virtually impossible to restyle, Hudson had to stick with the same shape through '54. The new stripped-down, lower-priced Pacemaker line included a sedan, two coupes, two-door brougham, and convertible. **2.** A Commodore Six four-door sedan cost $2282, but an Eight brought $84 more. **3.** "Step-down" meant occupants sat within the Monobilt frame, "with box-section steel-girder protection on all sides, even outside the rear wheels." Hudson promoted the safety aspect, and riders truly felt they were "stepping down" when entering the car. **4.** Heavy metal above the windshield made Hudson convertibles easy to spot. This is a Pacemaker Brougham, but open Hudsons also came in the Super Six series, and the Commodore Six and Eight. A hydraulic top was standard, power windows optional.

1

2

3

4

# 1950 Hudson

1. Lowest-priced Commodore Six was the $2257 club coupe, with a 123-horsepower, 262-cid engine. 2. Even in a Pacemaker, passengers had plenty of head and elbow room. Hudson seats were a whopping 64 inches wide. 3. Not only did a ragtop Commodore look glamorous, it claimed "the most room, best ride, and greatest safety of any American convertible." 4. Like most cars, Hudsons used coil springs up front. 5. Gentle-Acting rear leaf springs helped deliver a smooth highway ride. 6. Improved Center-Point steering was said to eliminate "wander" and help crosswind stability. 7. Pacemakers had a destroked version of the Super Six engine.

# Kaiser-Frazer Corporation

Kaiser-Frazer markets leftover 1949 models, until restyled '51s debut in spring of 1950

"Anatomic" '51s should have been ready, but glut of '49s forces Kaiser to give leftovers new serial numbers instead

All Kaisers and Frazers carry 226-cid six-cylinder Continental L-head engine

Thunderhead engines develop 112 horsepower except in Kaiser Special, which is rated 100 bhp

Kaiser Traveler continues after 1949 debut; has dual rear doors, like station wagon's tailgate

Vagabond is DeLuxe version of Kaiser Traveler

Handful of convertible sedans and four-door hardtops built

Kaiser Virginian four-door hardtop has nylon roof

Manhattan convertible sedan, the most opulent Frazer, has unique metal-framed glass pillars

Cofounder Joseph Frazer no longer is connected with the company, having departed in spring 1949

Henry Kaiser and son Edgar are in charge

Kaiser-Frazer ranks 12th in sales, with total of 146,911 units in calendar year

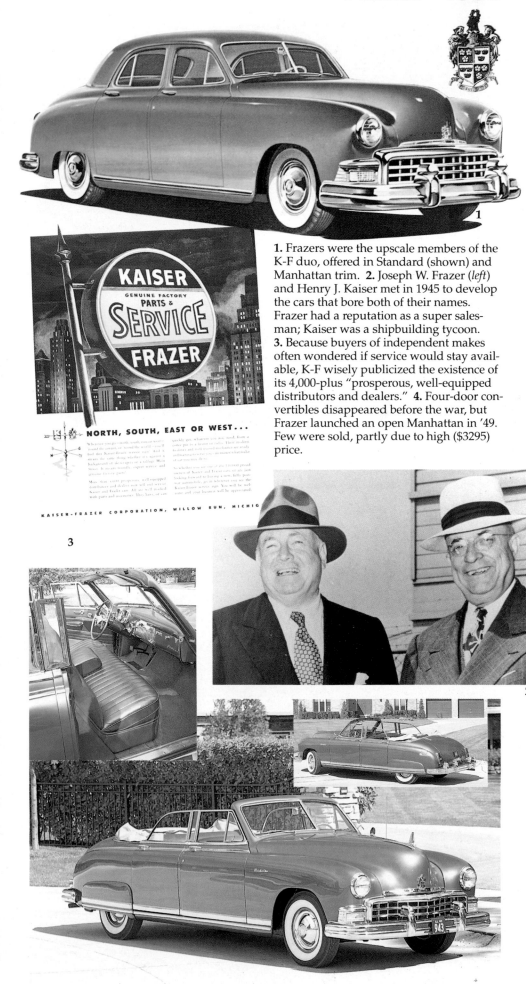

1. Frazers were the upscale members of the K-F duo, offered in Standard (shown) and Manhattan trim. 2. Joseph W. Frazer (*left*) and Henry J. Kaiser met in 1945 to develop the cars that bore both of their names. Frazer had a reputation as a super sales-man; Kaiser was a shipbuilding tycoon. 3. Because buyers of independent makes often wondered if service would stay avail-able, K-F wisely publicized the existence of its 4,000-plus "prosperous, well-equipped distributors and dealers." 4. Four-door con-vertibles disappeared before the war, but Frazer launched an open Manhattan in '49. Few were sold, partly due to high ($3295) price.

# 1950 Frazer

**1.** A Frazer four-door sedan cost $2395 in standard form (shown), or $200 more in fancier Manhattan guise, with Bedford cloth and nylon upholstery—or full leather. Their 112-horsepower, 226-cid Supersonic L-head six-cylinder engine was designed by Continental but built by K-F. **2.** Nearly 40 color combinations were available inside a Frazer. **3.** Frazer claimed its 27 cubic feet of luggage space was "half again as much as in most cars." On a long (123.5-inch) wheelbase, Frazers rode pleasantly and handled adeptly. **4.** Brightwork on the dashboard was common in the '50s. Frazer's speedometer and clock were identical in size, mounted ahead of a Clear-vision steering wheel.

**5.** Industrial designer Brooks Stevens penned a series of styling proposals for the 1950 Frazer—some of which suggest what became the '51 Kaiser. **6.** Note the slight windshield dip in this three-tone "Custom Sedan," which kept much of the original Frazer's sheetmetal. **7.** A full-width slot grille and wraparound back window mark this Stevens rendering. Engineers also pondered new engine alternatives.

# Kaiser 1950

1

**1.** Barely more than 15,000 Kaisers went on sale this season, as customers awaited fully redesigned models. Top seller was this DeLuxe sedan, although a Special cost $200 less. **2.** Dashboards featured a clock to match the speedometer, and a map light on the steering column shield. **3.** Kaiser seats promised "as much comfort space as your davenport at home." **4.** After styling the ill-fated 1948 Tucker, Alex Tremulis moved to Kaiser-Frazer, becoming head of advanced design. **5.** Ideas for '51 came from in-house teams, and from consultants Howard "Dutch" Darrin and Brooks Stevens. This Stevens concept has a slot grille formed into the bumper. **6.** Stevens's "Town Sedan" featured lower-body cladding. **7.** An oval grille would not be used, but the general shape of the 1951 Kaiser is evident.

2

3

5

6

4

7

# 1950 Kaiser

1

2

1. Practical-minded shoppers might choose a Kaiser DeLuxe Vagabond utility sedan (shown)—or the similar Special Traveler, for $200 less. Special engines made only 100 horsepower. 2. Symmetry was a major element of dashboard design. 3. The Vagabond's 10-foot cargo space was accessible via two hinged rear panels, with rear seat cushions folded. Note the slatted floor. 4. Long before other automakers got the idea, Kaiser offered a four-door hardtop—the $2995 Virginian.

3

4

# Nash Motors

Full-size cars change little in second year of Airflyte styling

Radical "upside-down-bathtub" design is mocked, but sells well

Nash's aerodynamic drag rating is best in the industry

Statesman with 85-bhp six replaces 600 series

Ambassador is top model, with 234.8-cid overhead-valve six

Uniscope puts all instruments—and most controls—into pod on steering column

All Airflytes have reclining front seatbacks; pneumatic mattresses can be ordered

Nash-Kelvinator president George Mason prepares a small car . . . Rambler, on 100-inch wheelbase with 82-horsepower six, is first volume-built American compact

Initial Ramblers come only in Landau Convertible form, followed by station wagon

Hydra-Matic transmission available in Ambassador; engine starts by lifting gearshift

Nash has top sales season ever, with 191,865 cars sold

Model-year output totals 171,782 cars, for 11th-place ranking

Only about 11,400 Ramblers built in first season, but sales soon will rise

1

2

4                                                              3

1. Those who didn't scoff at the contours of a "bathtub" Nash Airflyte found a lot to like in the Wisconsin automaker's unique fleet, including a comfortable interior, cushy ride, and novel features. This Ambassador Super sedan sold for $2064. Nash claimed 25-mpg economy from the 112-horsepower six-cylinder engine.  2. No other car on the road looked anything like a Nash, especially from the rear. Note the semi-concealed wheels at front and rear. Owners often endured smirks from folks who observed that Nash seats converted into beds. 3. Despite its aero shape, an Ambassador trunk held a fair supply of luggage.  4. A Statesman two-door plays up Nash's Airflyte styling theme. 5. Ambassadors rode a 121-inch wheelbase and differed from the shorter (112-inch) Statesman only from the cowl forward.

NOW—WITH AIRFLYTE CONSTRUCTION

*The Luxurious*
*Nash Ambassador*
**FOR 1950**

5

# 1950 Nash

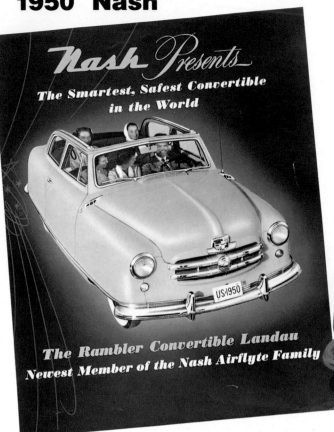

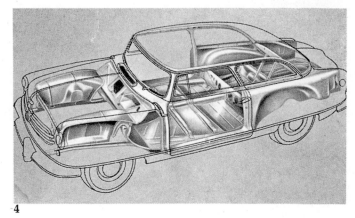

1. Other automakers had tinkered with small cars, but only Nash built one—mainly because president George Mason was intrigued by the concept of compacts. Rumored for months before its arrival in April 1950, the Rambler Landau was billed as "The Smartest, Safest Convertible in the World," promising the "safety of husky steel rails overhead." 2. Five fit snugly into a Rambler convertible. Mason knew that to survive as the seller's market eased, independents had to create cars that weren't offered by the Big Three. Note the broad cowl vent. 3. Rambler was the only open car on the market with fixed window frames and a slide-back top. 4. Nash claimed that the compact's version of unibodied Airflyte construction was "twice as rigid" as body-on-frame designs, "free of the usual squeaks and rattles." With a 100-inch wheelbase—15-inches shorter than Chevrolet's—Ramblers seemed to occupy a different world than their "bathtub" big brothers.

1

3

2

4

1. Two months after the convertible's debut came a Rambler Custom station wagon, for the same $1808 price. Ads claimed 30-mpg fuel economy—more with overdrive. 2. Ramblers were declared "a new beauty for the young in heart" that "steers like a dream, parks in a pocket." 3. Instruments sat in one cluster, ahead of the driver. A radio and Weather Eye Conditioned Air System were standard in the well-equipped Ramblers. 4. The 172.6-cid L-head engine was borrowed from the 1949 Nash 600. Light weight made Ramblers perky performers. 5. Big Nashes beckoned shoppers into this Oakland, California, dealership, but Ramblers were the wave of the future.

> 66 Won't there come a day when people will be concerned with the cost of doing things? 99
>
> *Nash-Kelvinator president* **George W. Mason**, *on the economic virtues of small-car ownership; October 1950*

5

# Packard Motor Car Company

Final season for Packard's "inverted-bathtub" shape

Late '49 and 1950 Packards show mild facelift of bulbous 1948-49 design

Twenty-Third Series of 1949-50 is known as "Golden Anniversary" Packard

Standard, Super Eight, and Custom Eight models marketed

Standard and DeLuxe Eight use 288-cid, 135-horsepower straight-eight

Super Eight engine is 327 cid and 150 bhp

Custom Eight's 356-cid straight-eight puts out 160 horsepower

Ultramatic is the only automatic transmission developed solely by an independent automaker

Ultramatic is standard on Custom series—lockup clutch gives no-slip cruising in direct drive

Rarely seen Station Sedan (wagon) uses structural wood only at tailgate

Model-year production dips to 42,627, for 15th-place ranking in industry

Company loses money, despite industry sales boom

Meager sales are attributed in part to loss of luxury image—neither midpriced nor costly Packards catch hold

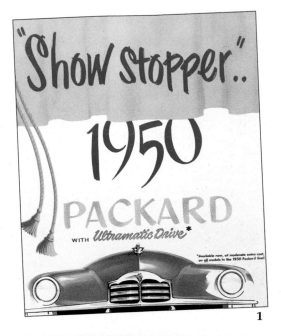

1. Packards came in three series: 135-bhp Eight; 150-bhp Super Eight, yielding a "limousine ride"; and top-drawer Custom Eight, said to be "built without regard for conventional 'price class' limitations." Impressive and award-winning a few years earlier, Packards now seemed painfully portly—often derided as "pregnant elephants." 2-3. Only 707 Custom Eight sedans were built, with a $3975 price tag and 356-cid engine. Extras included a spotlight and wind wings. 4. Even the standard Eight delivered a silken ride in a plush interior. Ultramatic cost $185, but this car is equipped with overdrive—a $92 extra. 5. A Super Eight DeLuxe club sedan cost $2894, but skipping DeLuxe trim saved $286.

"[Packard's nationwide dealer network] remains strong, its financial position never stronger and its product acceptance is rising to a new and promising peak."

*Packard president*
**Hugh J. Ferry**;
*December 1949*

NEW PACKARD *Ultramatic Drive*

The last word in automatic, no-shift control!

1. Packard issued only 77 Custom Eight convertibles, at an eye-popping $4520. An open Super Eight cost $1170 less. The mammoth Custom engine weighed half a ton.
2. Lowest-cost body was the standard Eight club sedan, shown in DeLuxe trim.
3. Standard on Custom Packards, optional on others, Ultramatic promised "no jerking, ever," and "no gasoline-wasting slippage."
4. Packard called its four-door Eights "touring sedans." 5. Even with 160 horsepower, Custom Eights set no speed records, as those ponies had to haul over 4300 pounds worth of Packard luxury.

"On top of the year just closed, which saw an all-time record reached in domestic shipments and a postwar production high of 104,593 [Packards], we foresee a 1950 output of upwards to 110,000 cars. This is dependent, of course, upon such factors as a steady flow of materials, continued good labor relationships, and an expanding economy."

*Packard president*
**Hugh J. Ferry**;
*January 1950*

# 1951 Chrysler

1

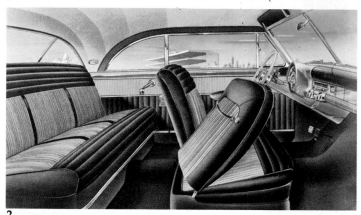

2

4

5

3

6

1. Imperials topped the Chrysler line, with "interiors of breath-taking elegance." 2. Newport hardtops had electric door windows, but crank-open quarter panes. 3. An Imperial convertible might have leather or leather/nylon upholstery. 4. Ads insisted that people of impeccable taste drove Imperials. 5. Chrysler dubbed the open Imperial "America's Smartest Car." 6. Fluid-Torque Drive added a torque converter to the Fluid-Matic unit, for quicker takeoffs.

THE 1951 DeSoto

1. All DeSotos, including this Custom sedan, wore a new grille and larger windshield. 2. A lower, but wider, rear window gave the DeSoto driver a wide-angle view. 3. Three circular gauge units graced the instrument panel. 4. DeLuxe and Custom DeSotos were said to be designed "expressly for you." The line included a club coupe, convertible, Sportsman hardtop, Suburban, and station wagon. 5. DeSoto's Carry-All utility sedan featured a fold-down rear seat. 6. The Carry-All's rear seatback and cushion folded to create a 6½ x 3½-foot cargo space. 7. Displacement of DeSoto's Powermaster six-cylinder engine grew to 251 cubic inches.

# 1951 Lincoln

**1.** Only 857 Cosmopolitan convertibles went on sale, priced at $3891 and tipping the scales at a burly 4615 pounds. Painted chartreuse, a well-loaded Cosmo was quite a sight. **2.** As before, Sport Sedans came in both standard Lincoln (shown) and top-of-the-line Cosmopolitan guise. *Motor Trend* named Lincoln "one of the best cars on the market." **3.** Lincoln's "sturdy, comfort-secure chassis" with "skyscraper braced cross members" promised "relaxing comfort . . . from the road up," allegedly filtering out fatigue-building vibration. The brawny InVincible 8 L-head engine produced 154 horsepower this year.

1. Cosmopolitans rode a wheelbase four inches longer than standard Lincolns, and cost considerably more—$629 more, in the case of the four-door Sport Sedan. Production of Cosmopolitan Sport Sedans shot up 47 percent, to 12,229. Unlike those on the smaller Lincoln, rear fenders did not protrude. 2. A padded roof gave the $3350 Cosmopolitan Capri some extra flair, but coupes failed to attract much attention in the marketplace. Only 2727 were built, in basic or Capri trim. Capris came in a choice of three colors, with harmonizing "vinyl-leather" roofs. Cosmopolitans added a full-length sidespear, replacing the controversial airfoil trim. 3. Capri interiors featured custom-tailored cord and leather upholstery. Formerly woodgrained, Lincoln dashboards now were painted to match the body color.

1

2

3

66 Statistics recently told us that Ford Motor Co. could produce about 6,300 cars a day. That was our total capacity—on paper. But that didn't stop us from boosting our production to nearly 9,000 units a day. . . . Now there's the difference between statistics and what actually can be done. 99

*Lincoln-Mercury general manager **Benson Ford**, on the tendency of statistical projections to underestimate American productivity; February 1951*

# 1951 Mercury

**1-2.** Like Lincoln, Mercury faced its final season in this "bathtub" form, adding a bolder grille and extended rear fenders with upright taillights. The longer, lower silhouette looked particularly pleasing in the club coupe body, which sold for $1947. Outside sun visors and fender skirts still were among the most popular extra-cost accessories. Mercury's V-8 engine added two horsepower (now 112). **3.** Browsers had plenty to choose from in Mercury showrooms, "styled just for you." The selection of models again included a Monterey coupe, with "vinyl-leather" or canvas top and leather or leather/cord interior. Newly optional Merc-O-Matic Drive featured a "natural" selector dial. Swiftest acceleration was attained by starting off in Low range, then shifting manually into Drive.

1

2

3

4

1. Least-popular Mercury model was the eight-passenger station wagon. Only 3812 were produced. Note the jumbo fender skirts and such extras as a grille guard, sun visor, and spotlight. 2. A Mercury Sport Sedan tows a float in the Santa Claus Parade down Chicago's State Street, on November 17, 1951. Partly because TV had not yet taken hold of kids' attention, parades often drew enormous crowds. 3. Mercury's four-door Sport Sedan was the most popular, with an even $2000 price and 157,648 produced. Many considered this year's brightwork and extra size excessive, detracting from the clean look of the 1949-50 models—especially the coupes. 4. Rear-fender script reveals that this convertible has the new Merc-O-Matic.

# 1951 Buick

## General Motors Corporation

Buicks get restyled front end

Hardtop joins Buick Special line

Buick drops to fourth in production, behind Plymouth

Final Cadillac Series 61 models built

Four Cadillac series on sale; all have Hydra-Matic

Chevrolets get slightly protruding rear fenders and cleaner-looking grille

All Oldsmobiles have V-8 engines, and switch from rear coils to rear leaf springs

Restyled Oldsmobiles win 20 of 41 stock-car starts

Super 88 joins Oldsmobile line, on new 120-inch wheelbase

Slow-selling Oldsmobile station wagons discontinued

Standard Olds 88, with Chevrolet bodyshell, includes only sedans

Self-winding watch available in Oldsmobile steering-wheel hub

Pontiacs come in 28 models—production is second-best ever, clinching fifth-place ranking

Four-door Pontiac fastbacks extinct . . . two-doors soon dropped

Pontiac marks 25th anniversary

1. A toned-down grille marked this year's "Smart Buy" Buicks. 2. Buick initially used the Riviera nameplate for four-door sedans as well as two-doors. This Roadmaster Riv went for $3044, with a 152-horsepower straight-eight. Roadmasters wore an ample quantity of chrome—but far more would be coming later in the decade. Two-tone paint sparked sales. 3. Not a strong seller, the Buick Roadmaster Estate wagon cost $3780. As usual, the ad copywriters stayed busy formulating lavish praise. Roadmasters, for instance, were described as the "brilliant master of the road in performance, prestige, and the sheer luxury of its travel."

1. Buick engineers helped design wild show cars, including the XP-300. Inside are Mr. and Mrs. C. E. Wilson, accompanied by chief engineer Charles Chayne. 2. Both the XP-300 and Le Sabre held an aluminum 215-cid V-8. Note the fine-toothed grille and teardrop headlight nacelles—styling touches coming in 1954. 3. GM used the XP-300 to promote other products. The supercharged engine used an AC oil filter. 4. Harley Earl, head of GM styling, sits behind the wheel of the LeSabre show car. 5. Buick Specials now carried the same size engine as Supers. 6. Convertibles came in all three Buick series.

# 1951 Packard

1

2

3

4

5

6

**1-2.** A Packard 250 Mayfair hardtop coupe was not only luxurious but colorful—even sporty in nature. Note the wraparound three-piece rear window, a feature on many makes. **3.** A gracefully winged hood ornament accented the lavish nature of a Mayfair—even if purists mourned the demise of ultra-posh Packards of the past. **4-5.** Only a four-door sedan was offered in the Patrician 400 series, with a 155-horsepower, 327-cid straight-eight and Ultramatic. Dressed in black, a $3662 Patrician suggested restrained elegance. **6.** A Packard and a Buick pulled up at the pumps of this Mobilgas station—which endured two competitors right across the street. Note the spouted water can for filling radiators—a frequent need of Fifties cars, especially as they aged.

# Studebacker Corporation

Studebaker Commanders and Land Cruisers get V-8 engine

V-8 displaces 232.6 cid and delivers 120 horsepower

Studebaker's is first overhead-valve V-8 from an independent, and first in low-price field—expected to spark sales

V-8 contributes to small-block engine technology—and helps topple price barrier between popular-priced and luxury cars

Engineers had considered overhead cams—even a hemi—but chose overhead-valve design

Commanders now ride Champion's shorter (115-inch) wheelbase—lose 200 pounds

Land Cruiser sedan drops from 124-inch to 119-inch span

Though criticized, "bullet-nose" look is popular, and draws considerable attention; second chrome circle is added

Automatic Drive available, after introduction during 1950

Overdrive-equipped Studebaker accelerates to 60 mph in less than 13 seconds

Studebaker is first auto manufacturer to install Orlon convertible tops

U.S. production drops to 246,195 in abbreviated model year; Stude ranks ninth

1. A procession of '51s looks nearly finished on the Studebaker assembly line.
2. Economy-oriented Champions stuck with their 169.6-cid L-head engine. This two-door sports bumper guards, wheel covers, and chrome window trim. 3. The new 120-horsepower Commander V-8 promised "a thrill for your throttle foot," as well as frugal running. Two V-8s with overdrive got better mileage than all eights and most standard sixes at the 1951 Mobilgas Run. 4. A Studebaker rear end peeks past the carport of a tract home—typical of 1950s suburban style.

# 1952

Despite the Korean War, Americans considered themselves to be prospering. They were, too, as judged by continually rising incomes and modest unemployment—down as low as three percent. Median family income approached $3900 a year, and the average full-time worker earned just over $3400—just about the price of a Packard convertible (or a pair of Fords). College teachers could expect about $5100 yearly, lawyers around $9000.

Three out of five families had a car, and two-thirds of homes had telephones. Already, one in three American households watched television—perhaps with one of the new TV trays propped in front of each family member. The traditional evening ritual of eating—and conversing—around the dinner table was in jeopardy.

The family automobile was turning into an *extension* of the home. More and more cars were loaded with comforts and conveniences, from power steering and sofa-plush seats to outside mirrors and even the new automatic-dimming headlights. Radios, on the other hand, were AM-only, just as they were in most homes, and nobody thought—yet—about playing music recordings in an automobile.

Some 56 million viewers saw vice-presidential candidate Richard Nixon's "Checkers" speech, in which he told of his 1950 car, mortgage, and "Republican cloth coat" for wife Pat. Dwight Eisenhower trounced Adlai Stevenson in the presidential election. TV premieres included *The Jackie Gleason Show*, Jack Webb's *Dragnet*, and the first *Today Show*, starring Dave Garroway.

Kay Starr sang "Wheel of Fortune," the Four Aces crooned "Tell Me Why," and Teresa Brewer waited "Till I Waltz Again With You." The "penny postcard" now cost a whopping two cents, but urban residents got two mail deliveries a day. The average American woman married at age 20, looking forward to a family—but seldom continuing in a career.

Fast-food restaurants had been scattered around the country for years, but Americans were taking a fresh interest in no-wait service. Some of the new drive-ins even had carhops to take orders right at car-side, and deliver the food on trays that hooked onto the open car window.

Gary Cooper won an Oscar for *High Noon*, Gene Kelly was *Singin' in the Rain*, and the comedy duo of Dean Martin and Jerry Lewis captured laughs from young moviegoers. Three-D glasses appeared, but neither that fad nor big-screen Cinerama would last more than a few years.

Anxious Americans began to scan the skies for (alleged) flying saucers, entertain themselves with new Paint-by-Numbers kits, or peruse *Mad* magazine. Travelers might stay at one of the new Holiday Inns. On a less pleasant note, the scourge of polio hit more than 50,000, subversives were barred from teaching in public schools, and unions—including auto workers—were accused of harboring "Reds."

The Korean conflict placed a limit on auto production. As a rule, most automakers were restricted to 80 percent of their output in 1950. The National Production Authority set a specific limit of 4,342,000 cars, and actual calendar-year output turned out to be just a few thousand under that figure. Price ceilings were in effect, too.

Cadillac upped the output of its V-8 to 190 horsepower, complete with dual exhausts. Ford launched an overhead-valve six, Lincoln got a new ohv V-8, and Hudson adopted Twin H-Power (a fancy designation for twin carburetors).

Ford came out with a totally redesigned line of cars, while each rival made do with facelifts. Shoppers could even buy a car at Sears: the new Allstate, a thinly-disguised clone of the Henry J.

More than two million automatic transmissions were installed, despite a temporary limit, early in the model year, on the number of cars that could have automatic. One-third of cars had a V-8 engine. Sixes would hang on for many more years, but straight-eights were nearing the end of their era. Automotive gadgets proliferated, as aftermarket manufacturers had their inventors ponder more and more comforts and conveniences.

At a typical gas station, regular fuel cost about a quarter a gallon—considerably more than today, when allowance is made for inflation. In May, government limits on credit were dropped, with 24-month finance terms seen likely. Dealers anticipated a serious upswing in sales if customers could spread their payments over a longer period.

No new models debuted until November '51, and many waited until early 1952. Some experts recommended a return to autumn launches, which had been the rule before World War II.

State license plates came in 34 lengths and 15 heights, and Charles Chayne of GM called for a standard size. Fort Worth, Texas, proposed banning cars to create a pedestrian shopping mall. That change didn't happen, but it served as a portent for the future.

Crosley production ceased in July, as the company merged into General Tire and Rubber. Americans bought the occasional imported minicar, but home-grown minis weren't yet in demand. As usual, several more independents—Autoette, Skorpion, Woodill—tried their hand, but few survived.

Prosperous or not, Americans weren't able—or willing—to snap up everything the automakers produced. In contrast to the recent past, when they were able to sell every last vehicle the factories turned out—with a hefty profit—dealers were seeing cars languish on the lots. Kaiser, in fact, touched up thousands of leftover '51s and remarketed them as '52 models, until a mildly redesigned replacement was ready.

In some dealers' minds—and in the plans of certain Detroit executives—the answer to a buyer's market was obvious: Sell 'em hard, and move the merchandise at any cost. The industry was preparing for a sales blitz, a full-scale assault on the consumer led by Ford and Chevrolet, whose repercussions are still felt today.

# Chrysler Corporation

Mild facelifts given to '52 models, which differ little in styling or technical details

Chrysler, DeSoto, and Dodge continue to offer only *semi*-automatic shifting

Imperial series retrenches a bit by dropping its convertible coupe

Traveler utility wagons depart from Chrysler lineup . . . final Saratogas on sale

Windsor sixes can get Hydraguide power steering . . . all Chryslers may have electric windows and tinted glass

Six-cylinder Chrysler engine gains three horsepower; Hemi stands pat at 180 bhp

FireDome Hemi V-8 power now available in DeSotos—only the tiny Crosley engine produces more horsepower per cubic inch

DeSoto V-8 with 160 horsepower is produced in new plant

Dodge Wayfarer line trimmed to two models . . . roadster gone

Plymouth clings to Number Three production position, followed by Buick and Pontiac . . . Dodge remains in seventh spot

*Motor Trend* magazine awards V-8 Chrysler the title of "Best Engineered" car

Chrysler exhibits experimental Ghia-built C-200 convertible, evolved from K-310 coupe . . . other show cars follow, most powered by Hemi V-8 engines

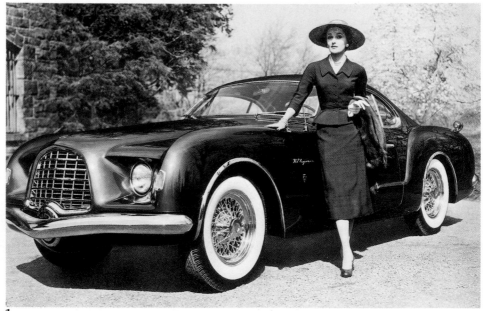

1

2

1. One of a series of Chrysler "idea cars" in the early '50s, the D'Elegance coupe followed an earlier K-310. On a cut-down New Yorker platform, its "2+1" body held a sideways rear seat. 2. Like most Chrysler "dream cars" of the period, the Special was designed by a team under Virgil Exner and built by the Ghia company in Italy. Note the snug spare-tire compartment. 3-4. An open companion to the K-310 coupe, the C-200 show car also rode a stock Saratoga chassis. Distinctive "gunsight" taillights would be seen again on 1955-56 Imperials. Full wheel cutouts were a typical Exner styling touch. Both the K-310 and C-200 were considered for production, but rejected. Note the dual exhaust pipes.

3

4

1

2

4

> 66 Chrysler designers have avoided throwing practical considerations to the wind merely to achieve fantastic styling for styling's sake. 99
>
> *Chrysler vice president of engineering and research* **J. C. Zeder**, *on Chrysler's C-200 show car; March 1952*

**1-2.** Chrysler's Ghia-built, one-of-a-kind show cars didn't always disappear after their debuts. This fastback Special coupe was updated by the factory during its three-year active life by replacing its original semi-automatic transmission with PowerFlite. After 1955, it was released from active service. The body is aluminum from the cowl back, with steel front fenders and an aluminum hood. Chrysler's 331-cid Hemi V-8 powered most show cars of the period. **3.** Chrysler advertisements focused on the fashionable show cars: (*top to bottom*) K-310, C-200, Special, and D'Elegance. **4.** Occupants of this Ghia-built coupe could swivel into position. Note the large round gauge units, and the seatbelt buckle—safety belts were rare except on race cars.

3

# 1952 Chrysler

1-2. Like other Chrysler products, the New Yorker Newport hard-top changed little for '52, but backup lights sat below taillights. 3. Steering wheels matched the upholstery, ahead of a large instrument cluster. 4. Customers had a smaller selection of "Beautiful Chrysler" models to choose from. 5-6. A New Yorker convertible cost $4093 and weighed 4450 pounds. 7. Lowest-cost Saratoga was the club coupe, at $3187. 8. The Hemi V-8 in a Saratoga sent its 180 horses to Fluid-Torque Drive. 9. The Town & Country name now identified a Saratoga station wagon. 10. New Yorkers rode a longer wheelbase than Saratogas and six-cylinder Windsors.

## Cunningham Shifts from Racing to Limited Production

Famed sportsman Briggs Cunningham sent a series of fast roadsters to the Le Mans race. Note the four carbs on the Chrysler Hemi V-8. Only a handful of Italian-built race-and-ride C-3 fastback coupes went on sale, at $9000 each. Three C-4R Cunninghams ran at Le Mans, as Briggs himself drove to a fourth-place finish.

1. DeSoto got its own version of the Hemi engine. Named FireDome, this scaled-down 276.1-cid V-8 yielded 160 horsepower—20 fewer than Chrysler's, but equal to the output of the new Lincoln. 2. DeSoto sponsored Groucho Marx's popular quiz show, *You Bet Your Life*. On radio or TV, major entertainers typically had a single sponsor, cleverly weaving the brand name into scripts. 3. Only a fingertip might be needed for parking, but power steering gave the driver little road "feel."

# 1952 Plymouth

**1.** Plymouth touted 46 improvements, most of them hidden. They included modified springs/shocks, revised starting and braking hardware, plus easier shifting. A new rear nameplate, integrated with the trunk handle, replaced the former script. Style leader was the Cranbrook Belvedere hardtop, at $2216. **2.** Fabrics blended with the instrument panel and door panels in Tone-Tailored interiors. Solex safety glass was optional. Note the flat two-piece windshield and the plaid seat covers—a popular add-on. **3.** Do-it-yourselfers in thousands of driveways could install new Champion plugs—and handle tuneups of the easy-to-service L-head engine.

1

3

2

**1.** No other manufacturer offered a two-tone paint scheme similar to that of the Plymouth Belvedere. **2.** Most Plymouth improvements were beneath the surface. President D. S. Eddins promised "the most gentle ride, the smoothest engine performance and the greatest safety ever built into a car for the lowest price field." **3.** Overdrive engaged as the driver's foot lifted off the gas pedal at 25 mph or more.

## Crosley Motors, Inc.

Lineup continues with little change; even some prices remain the same

Cooperative development with Union Pacific Railroad produces shipping boxcar that can hold 16 Crosleys

Power again comes from 44-cid four-cylinder engine with cast iron block

Only 2075 Crosleys are built in 1952 model year as automobile production halts in July

Final tally includes 358 Hotshot and Super Sports roadsters—still able to make strong showings on race courses

Crosley Motors is acquired by General Tire and Rubber Company, which gets controlling interest for about $60,000

Corporate assets amount to $5,728,208 at time of sale

Powel Crosley, Jr., has spent $3 million in a valiant attempt to stay afloat

Reasons for failure include trend away from no-frills transport in the "Bigger is Better" Fifties

America has shown it isn't yet ready for a domestic minicar

Crosley engine remains in production, used in power boats and for portable refrigeration

Ralph Roberts and Jack Wills develop kit to transform a Crosley sedan or station wagon into shapely Skorpion sports car

1

1. Jingle contests were popular pastimes. Thousands of Americans took pen in hand to compose rhapsodic prose about a product—typically, 25 words or less—hoping to win a valuable prize. In this challenge sponsored by Mission Orange soda pop, young folks simply had to write the last line. Top prizes: an orange grove and Crosley Super Sports roadster. 2. Crosley was represented at the Chicago Auto Show by this Super convertible, priced at $1059.

2

# Ford Motor Company

Ford Motor Company is only automaker to fully restyle all its cars this year

Fords get overhead-valve Mileage Maker six-cylinder engine . . . flathead Strato-Star V-8 adds 10 horsepower

Fords come in three series: Mainline, Customline, Crestline

All-steel Ford station wagons debut, including woody-look Country Squire

Country Sedan and Crestlines come only with V-8 engines

Veteran road-tester Tom McCahill calls totally restyled '52 "the best looking Ford ever built"

Hardtop coupe now available in Lincoln and Mercury lines

Lincoln adds ball-joint front suspension and 317.5-cid overhead-valve V-8 engine for restyled Cosmopolitan and Capri

Power steering and four-way power seat available on Lincolns

Mercury V-8 boosted to 125 bhp, via higher compression and improved carburetion

Overdrive-equipped Mercury wins class in Mobilgas Economy Run

Lincolns take top four spots in 2000-mile *Carrera Panamericana* road race, beating Ferraris, Chryslers—and Hudson Hornets

Continental 195X "Car of Tomorrow" holds phone, dictaphone, automatic jacks

1

2

3

1. Helmsmen of Ford Motor Company included Lincoln-Mercury chief Benson Ford (*third from left*), executive vice president Ernest R. Breech (*fifth from left*), and president Henry Ford II (*sixth from left*). 2. Led by George Snyder and Tom Hibberd, these artists at work on a full-scale rendering of the 1952 Ford were close to the final design. The basic shape—boxy lower body with fenders near hood-height—was decided fairly early in the process, which began in 1949. 3. A few redesigned '52s get final inspection.

# 1952 Ford

1. Three Crestline models topped the Ford line, including this $2027 Sunliner convertible. 2. In the mid-range Customline series, a Tudor sedan cost $1570. Customlines sold best, by far. 3. Country Sedan station wagons had plain bodysides, while the higher-priced Country Squire wore simulated wood. 4. Ford originally was to get an overhead-valve V-8, like Lincoln's, but that would have to wait. 5. Ford issued 77,320 hardtops in the new shape. This Crestline Victoria sports such extras as full-disc hubcaps, skirts, Continental kit, and dual exhausts. 6. Without add-ons, a Victoria cost $1925. Ford-O-Matic added $170. 7. Owners loved dealer-installed and aftermarket goodies. This Sunliner has oversize V-8 emblems, rocker moldings, grille guard, and more. 8. Not many young fellows enjoyed service of this sort at the local Sohio station.

## 1952 FORD MODELS

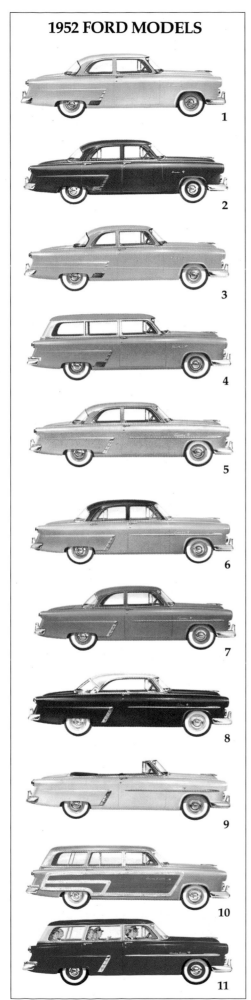

1. Mainline Tudor sedan. 2. Mainline Fordor sedan. 3. Mainline business coupe.
4. Mainline Ranch Wagon. 5. Customline Tudor sedan. 6. Customline Fordor sedan.
7. Customline club coupe. 8. Crestline Victoria hardtop coupe. 9. Crestline Sunliner convertible. 10. Crestline Country Squire. 11. Customline Country Sedan. 12. This Customline Tudor served the Houston Police Department. 13. Ford's new six developed 101 horsepower. 14. A series of contests sponsored by soap companies gave away 20 Fords. 15. Note the hooded gauge cluster in this Victoria.

# 1952 Oldsmobile

1

2

3

1. Breathing through a Quadri-Jet carburetor, output of Oldsmobile's fabled Rocket V-8 engine rose to 160 horsepower. Hydra-Matic added a second range for hill climbing and peak performance. DeLuxe 88s had the Super's body, but a 145-bhp V-8 engine. **2.** Olds promised a Custom-Lounge "Rocket Ride" with "deep-decked comfort." **3.** Roomy back seats featured "rich, durable fabrics in a choice of harmonizing colors." A new rear stabilizer helped handling. **4.** Wheelbases of Ninety-Eight models grew by two inches, perhaps accounting for the promised "ultra-long look." The big convertible cost $3229. **5.** A $3022 Ninety-Eight hardtop sold better than the convertible. Power steering allowed "1 finger" parking.

EVERY INCH A

## classic!

(and 213 inches over-all!)

It's *long* on looks—nearly eighteen feet of modern classic styling. It's *a dream for riding comfort*—thanks to the new longer wheelbase that *floats* you over choppy roads. It's *a rocket for performance!* 160 horsepower "Rocket" Engine with new Oldsmobile Hydra-Matic Super Drive.* Parking? That's a *breeze* with nearly 80% of the steering effort supplied by GM Hydraulic Steering*!

It's a *Classic* . . . the fabulous Ninety-Eight featuring Oldsmobile's latest contribution to supreme comfort: *Custom-Lounge Cushions.*"

It's yours to try—*now!*

*Hydra-Matic Super Drive, GM Hydraulic Steering, Custom-Lounge Cushions optional at extra cost. Equipment, accessories, and trim illustrated subject to change without notice.

Oldsmobile Ninety-Eight Holiday Coupé. A General Motors Product.

"ROCKET"

# OLDSMOBILE *Ninety-Eight*

5

Tomorrow's Classic

Oldsmobile Ninety-Eight Convertible. A General Motors Product.    *Hydra-Matic Super Drive, GM Hydraulic Steering, Autronic-Eye, white sidewall tires (when available) optional at extra cost. Equipment, accessories, and trim illustrated subject to change without notice.

This is the climax of the "classic" idea in motor cars! This is the car that brings the "ultra-long look" to the convertible field—the Oldsmobile *Ninety-Eight!* Here, for you, is a new measure of grace and glamor and low-poised beauty in an automobile. Interiors are the richest in Oldsmobile history—luxurious long-wearing leather over deep-foam rubber, sparkling new trim, beautiful new color combinations! And above all, this is a "Rocket" Engine car —powered by Oldsmobile's famous new 160-horsepower engine! Paired with new Hydra-Matic Super Drive*, the "Rocket" brings you a thrilling new kind of smooth, effortless action. GM Hydraulic Steering* and the exciting new Autronic-Eye* make driving easier and safer than ever! Drive tomorrow's classic—the Oldsmobile *Ninety-Eight* Convertible Coupé! It's yours today at your Oldsmobile dealer's!

"ROCKET"

# OLDSMOBILE

*Ninety-Eight*

4

## 1952 OLDSMOBILE SUPER 88 and DELUXE 88 MODELS

1. Most popular Olds was the four-door Super 88. 2. Super 88 convertible. 3. Super 88 Holiday hardtop. 4. Super 88 two-door sedan. 5. Club coupe was the lowest-priced Super 88. 6. Cheapest Olds was the DeLuxe 88 two-door. 7. DeLuxe 88 four-door sedan. 8. Super 88 four-door. 9. Motorists saw few roads other than two-lanes in mid-America. Here, an Olds and Pontiac approach an intersection outside of East Peoria, Illinois. Note the Skelly gas sign and roadside fruit market.

## White Castle— Fast Food Pioneer, Still Going Strong

In 1921, Walter Anderson opened the first White Castle restaurant in Wichita, Kansas. Its specialty: small-scale burgers and trimmings—in a hurry. Patrons were encouraged to "Buy 'em by the sack." This White Castle outlet stood on South Western Avenue, in Chicago. White Castle still grills "sliders" today, their little burgers being loved by millions. Other early fast-food emporiums— Twinburger, Henry's, Chicken in the Rough—faded after a time. Already, in many parts of the U.S., drive-ins were becoming the favored meeting spot for teenagers.

# Hudson Motor Car Company

Hudson launches Wasp series, replacing Super Six

Full line also includes Pacemaker, Hornet, and Commodore Six and Eight

Hornets come in four body styles, with minor revisions in grille and body trim

All models get revised trim details, and all can have Hydra-Matic transmission—including budget-priced Pacemaker

Twin H-Power, featuring dual carburetors, arrives as option during '52 model year

Dual carbs available on all sixes, but mainly installed on Hornets, boosting their already-strong performance

Hudson promises "jet-like acceleration" from Twin H-Power engine

Marshall Teague wins 12 of 13 stock-car events at wheel of Hudson Hornet . . . Hudsons also claim 27 NASCAR victories

Tim Flock wins 250-mile Detroit race in Twin H-Power Hornet . . . Hudsons also take second and third

Ads push Hudson's stock-car race record

Model-year output drops to lowest level since 1942—just over half are Hornets

Aging "Step-down" design still revered for superior handling characteristics and roadability on the highway

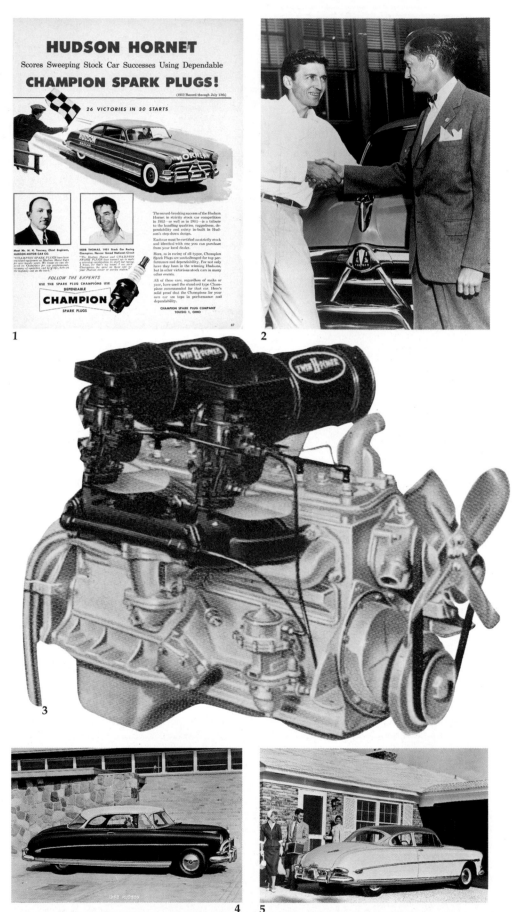

1. Even parts manufacturers took advantage of the hot Hornet's racing prowess for their advertising messages. 2. Tim Flock (*left*), youngest of the "Flying Flock" brothers, picked up a new Hudson Hornet at the Detroit factory, greeted by assistant sales manager Roy Chapin, Jr. 3. Every Twin H-Power engine sported bright red air cleaners. 4. The new Wasp mixed a Pacemaker platform with the old Super Six's 262-cid engine. 5. At $2742, the club coupe was the cheapest—and lightest weight—Hornet. Note the long trunk lid and wraparound back window.

1

1. "Road handling," insists this two-tone Hornet sedan's owner, was "second to none in its day." With a 145-bhp, 308-cid six-cylinder engine, the four-door sold for $2769. Hydra-Matic cost extra. 2. Chicago's Courtesy Motors ranked as the country's largest Hudson dealer. Owner Jim Moran appeared regularly in the dealership's TV commercials and generated a long series of innovative promotions that pushed sales to the limit. Even the roof held Hudsons, as customers arrived in throngs to scan the newest Hornets. Car-shopping was becoming a major family event. 3. Hornets got the most publicity, but Hudson had a full range of cars, from the thrifty Pacemaker and fresh Wasp to the last Commodore Eights. 4. This dealership operated by M.L. "Red" Townsend used plenty of neon for its signage and decoration.

2

3

4

# 1952 Studebaker

## Studebaker Corporation

Studebaker celebrates 100th anniversary—still turning out vehicles mainly in South Bend, Indiana

Unibodied "N-Series" with evolutionary bullet nose is developed, then abandoned, due to government restraints and growing military production

Studebaker joins pillarless hardtop ranks with new Starliner body style

Final facelift hits 1947-51 bodyshells, prior to all-new 1953 model

Bullet-nose front ends gone, replaced by wraparound split grille ahead of longer, lower hood

Studebakers take two class wins at Mobilgas Economy Run: 27.8 mpg for Champion, 25.6 mpg for Commander V-8

Car/truck volume slips to 231,837 units in slowdown year for the industry

Studebaker maintains ninth-place ranking in American passenger-car production

Corporate earnings set records at $586 million, but profits amount to only $1.4 million

Commander convertible paces Indianapolis 500 race

Indy event is preceded by parade of 25 historic vehicles, led by float with Conestoga wagon, in "Caravan of the Century"

Race victor Troy Ruttman takes home the pace car—plus prize money

**1-2.** Finally, Studebaker issued the increasingly popular hardtop coupe body style. The Commander State Starliner with V-8 engine started at $2488, but a six-cylinder Champion ran $268 less. This overdrive-equipped Commander Starliner sports a gas-door guard, full wheel discs, and two-tone paint (for the first time). **3.** Starliner hardtops sold well, in both "sprightly" Champion and potent Commander guise, accounting for 15 percent of Studebaker's total. "Sparkling with verve and vigor in every line," the brochure insisted, "it's a remarkable gas saver . . . free from power wasting excess weight." Upholstery was fabricated in button-tufted nylon or optional leather. Each Champion body style came in three trim levels: Custom, DeLuxe, or Regal.

1

2

3

4

5

6

**1.** Studebaker began as a wagon maker, as shown in this centennial ad. **2.** Stude was hardly alone in tying design themes to "jets," even though most planes were propeller-driven. **3.** Soon-to-be President Eisenhower paraded in a Commander. **4.** From left, designers Robert Bourke, Raymond Loewy, and Holden Koto pose with a prototype of the Champion Starlight coupe. **5.** Frugal operation was always a top selling point. **6.** First Studebaker of the second century leaves the plant on February 18, 1952.

# Ford Motor Company

Ford celebrates 50th anniversary on June 16 . . . festivities include special *Ed Sullivan Show* and dedication of Engineering and Research Center

Ford distributes two million Norman Rockwell calendars and publishes book *Ford at Fifty*

Ford production comes within 100,000 of Chevrolet's 1.35 million cars . . . Mercury output soars, but fails to overtake Oldsmobile and Dodge

Flathead V-8 engine in final season

Sales blitz underway as Ford chases Chevrolet: cars go to dealers whether ordered or not . . . discounting is rampant, hard-sell promotions common

Ford Sunliner convertible paces Indianapolis 500 race, driven by William Clay Ford; limited run of replicas built

Power brakes and steering available on Fords, starting in mid-season; also available on Lincoln-Mercury models

Ford six with overdrive gets 27.03 mpg at Mobilgas Run

Lincoln V-8 boosted to 205 horsepower, with four-barrel carburetion

Lincoln offers four-way power seat—an industry "first" . . . power windows offered, too

Lincolns take first four spots in Mexican Road Race—again

1. A mid-range Ford Customline sedan, said the sales brochure, was "big in size and long on beauty." 2. A Customline club coupe was "smart for two—with room for six." 3. Mainline Fords lacked the bright-work of Customline and Crestline, but offered the same styling and technical features. 4. Each year, automakers came up with lists of new features—some worthy, others not. Ford promoted an array of "Worth More" qualities, valuable not only while the car was new, but when it came time to resell.

**'53's leader is the '53 Ford !**

With 41 "Worth More" features it's worth more when you buy it... worth more when you sell it... the new STANDARD of the AMERICAN ROAD

See it...Value Check it...Test Drive it !

## Lightweight Sports Car Packs V-8 Punch

Well-known for its work with fiberglass, the Glasspar Company of Santa Ana, California, began building two-seat sports car bodies in 1950. Though most of the approximately 200 G-2s sold through 1955 were in kit form, a tubular steel frame was eventually made available, and Glasspar sold some completed versions powered by Ford and Mercury V-8s. Note the roll bar and separate monocle-like windscreens.

1

2

3

**1.** Like most hardtop coupes, Ford's $1941 Crestline Victoria looked best when two-toned. The sales brochure called it "sedan snug—convertible smart." **2.** The $2043 Crestline Sunliner convertible featured a Breezeway top with large zip-out window. **3.** Switching from an eight-passenger car to a cargo carrier took a claimed three minutes with a Ford Crestline Country Squire station wagon. Center seats folded into the floor. Body panels were trimmed with genuine maple or birch wood. Ford also offered a plain-bodyside Customline Country Sedan. **4.** Ford's K-bar frame, with deep channel struts, delivered added twist resistance. A variable-rate rear suspension used extra-long springs, and Hydra-Coil front springs were tailored to model weight. **5.** A view through the windshield demonstrated the value of Full-Circle visibility. Steering wheel hubs held a 50th-anniversary medallion. **6.** Ford's Mileage Maker six gave 101 horsepower. **7.** In its final season, the Strato-Star flathead V-8 delivered 110 bhp.

4

5

6

7

> ❝ Wait until the figures are in for this fourth quarter. We have some pretty nasty things in store for Chevrolet. ❞
>
> *Unidentified **Ford spokesman**, on the anticipated Ford sales victory over Chevy during the month of October 1953; November 1953*

# 1953 Lincoln

1

2

1. A Lincoln Capri hardtop not only felt luxurious, it looked rakish—especially viewed from down low. Even so, Lincoln continued to lag far behind Cadillac in popularity. 2. A 205-horsepower V-8 drove the $3226 Cosmopolitan sedan and every other model—45 more horses than in '52, and just five short of Cadillac's output. 3. Lincoln unflinchingly promoted the virtues of its vehicles for women, noting that the "smallest lady can fit easily" and "power brakes respond to the touch of a ballet slipper." No automaker today would promise to give "feminine hands control they've never known before." 4. The top-selling Capri hardtop cost $3549, with standard Hydra-Matic. Newly optional power steering also came from General Motors.

3

4

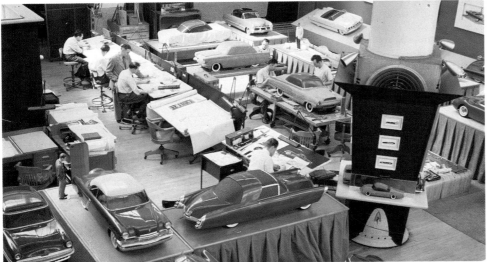

1. A fleet of pre-production '53s drove in the Mexican Road Race. Lincoln eagerly promoted its cars' impressive showings, as well as a first-in-class finish at the Mobilgas Economy Run. 2. Bob Estes was chief driver in the *Carrera Panamericana*. 3. Engines of Lincolns in the Mexican race were fitted with Champion spark plugs. Naturally, Champion suggested that owners of other cars might expect similar performance. 4. Stylists stayed busy not only with production Lincolns, but created Ford's show cars. 5. Three Ford brothers pose with a pair of dream cars: Henry Ford II in foreground, alongside the Continental Fifty-X; and in the rear, Benson Ford and William Clay Ford with the XL-500. 6. The front portion of the Fifty-X top retracted automatically into the rear. Gadgetry included automatic jacks. 7. By 1953, the family automobile—plain or plush—was a major part of "modern living," and everyone was presumed to want to "leave the past far behind."

# 1953 Oldsmobile

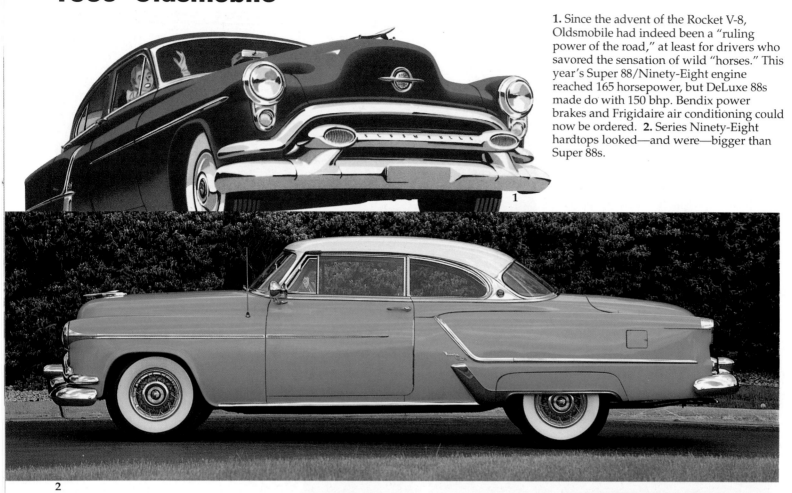

**1.** Since the advent of the Rocket V-8, Oldsmobile had indeed been a "ruling power of the road," at least for drivers who savored the sensation of wild "horses." This year's Super 88/Ninety-Eight engine reached 165 horsepower, but DeLuxe 88s made do with 150 bhp. Bendix power brakes and Frigidaire air conditioning could now be ordered. **2.** Series Ninety-Eight hardtops looked—and were—bigger than Super 88s.

**3.** Vying for attention against Cadillac's Eldorado and Buick's Skylark, Oldsmobile launched a limited-edition Ninety-Eight Fiesta convertible with panoramic windshield and 170-horsepower engine. Only 458 customers got one, for $5717. Its distinctive spinner wheel covers soon appeared as aftermarket add-ons. **4.** Ads still asked readers to "Make a date" with a Rocket Olds. **5.** A Ninety-Eight could get Safety-Padding atop its symmetrical dashboard. A new Quick-View Hydra-Matic quadrant sat below the speedometer.

MOST *Glamorous* CAR TO DATE !

MAKE A DATE WITH A "ROCKET 8"

OLDSMOBILE

1

2

3

1. Oldsmobile pushed both the glamour and comfort of the Ninety-Eight, which featured new squared-off seatbacks and Custom-Lounge cushions. 2. Two-tone upholstery was common in 1953 models, including the Super 88. 3. Oldsmobile called its new front end the "power look." Shown is a Super 88 sedan. 4. Super 88s blended the more potent V-8 with a smaller body—resulting in greater performance. 5. Oldsmobile officials celebrated the production of the company's four-millionth car in May of 1953. 6. This AC ad spotlighted the experimental Olds Starfire, with a 200-horsepower V-8 and 9:1 compression. AC spark plugs had been used on all Oldsmobiles since 1911.

4

5

6

Firing THE **OLDSMOBILE** Starfire

And Factory Equipment On Every Oldsmobile Since 1911

**AC SPARK PLUGS**

# 1953 Pontiac

**1-2.** Pontiac was attempting to shed its stodgy image. New styling on a longer wheelbase helped, but continued use of the familiar inline L-head engines did not. Continental spare tires, shown on a top-of-the-line Custom Catalina hardtop, were gaining a modest following as extra-cost accessories. Subtle rear-fender kick-ups gave a suggestion of tailfins. **3.** Buyers could pay extra to get illumination for the Indian-head hood ornament. **4.** All Pontiacs, including the Chieftain DeLuxe convertible, came with either a 239.2-cid six or 268.4-cid eight. The six produced 115/118 horsepower (manual/automatic), the eight, 118/122. Twin spotlights weren't standard fare. **5.** Only $66 separated the DeLuxe Catalina hardtop (shown) from a costlier Custom model. **6.** Even a practical-minded Pontiac sedan delivery looked good in two colors with DeLuxe bodyside trim.

1

2

3

4

5

6

1

2

3

6

4

5

**1.** In addition to a new wraparound windshield, Pontiacs had panoramic back windows. **2.** Pontiac continued to extol the economic virtues and dependable operation of its 26-model Chieftain lineup. Six- and eight-cylinder engines now differed only slightly in horsepower (the six gaining about 15 bhp this year), but eights delivered considerably more torque. **3-4.** Station-wagon fanciers could choose from a full dozen Pontiacs, including this woodgrained DeLuxe Eight. **5.** Pontiac's offering at the GM Motorama was this Parisienne town car. **6.** Outside, the Parisienne looked more stock than some show cars, but bucket-style seats and super-plush carpeting weren't like those fitted to any production Pontiacs.

# 1954 Plymouth

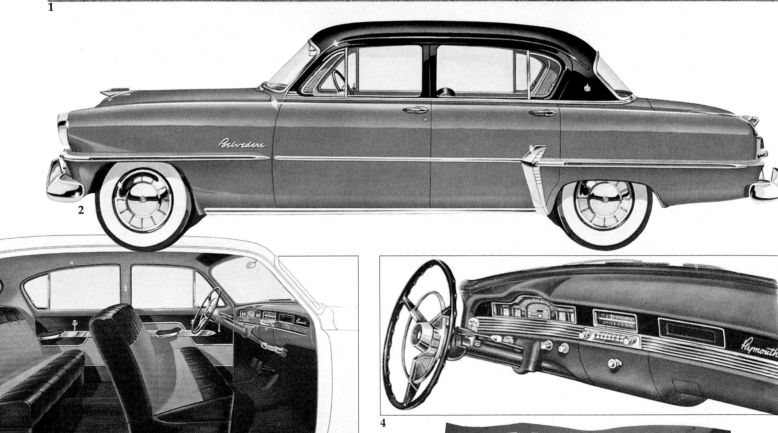

1. Belvedere replaced Cranbrook as the top-of-the-line Plymouth series. A Belvedere convertible, shown in Santa Rosa Coral, cost $2301. 2. Four body styles made up the Belvedere line, with tiny chrome fins atop rear fenders. 3. "Color-Tuned" styling gave Belvederes an interior that matched body hues. 4. Plymouth described the upper dashboard panel's enameling as a "soft, leather-like, no-glare finish." 5. Dealers needed plenty of friends to counteract the slow sales year. For the first time since 1931, Plymouth dropped below third place in calendar-year production—though the model-year total was strong enough to retain a Number Three ranking.

PLYMOUTH
AUTHORIZED
SALES · SERVICE
THAT MAKES FRIENDS

1. Formerly named Cambridge, budget-priced Plymouths now wore Plaza badges. Bare-bones model was was the business coupe, with a minimal $1618 sticker. Stripped-down cars attracted a certain following—and not just for use by salesmen and business travelers. 2. The Plaza four-door sedan cost $1765, versus $1873 for a Savoy and $1953 for a Belvedere. 3. Savoy was Plymouth's new mid-range series, shown in club coupe guise. 4. This is a Plaza station wagon, but two-door Suburbans came in all three Plymouth series. 5. Plymouth continued to focus on value in its advertising—but also on comfort and color harmony. Note the contrasting-color panel on the upper door of the Belvedere hardtop—now called a Sport Coupe. Hy-Drive was optional at first, but PowerFlite became available at midyear. So did a new higher-powered (110-bhp), 230.2-cid PowerFlow engine. Power steering could be ordered for the first time, but like all Chrysler units, the system lacked much road "feel." 6. Corporate president Lester L. "Tex" Colbert feels the exhaust of Chrysler's first turbine car—a Plymouth Belvedere. Exhaust heat was no longer an obstacle, as a regenerator recovered heat from exhaust gases, reducing fuel consumption as it improved cooling.

# 1954 Lincoln

1-2. Raising the price of a Lincoln Capri convertible by $332 doubtless didn't help sales. Only 1951 were built this year. Sheetmetal did not change, but the grille looked bolder, new full-length upper body-side chrome spears sat higher, and integrated tail/backup lights brought up the rear. 3. Instruments across the upper panel now sat against a gold background making them more difficult to read. All models had Hydra-Matic, with its shift quadrant in a band above the steering wheel hub. 4. Lincoln's V-8 engine still put out 205 horsepower—less than Cadillac or Chrysler—at a time when power boosted sales. 5. A total of 13,598 Capri four-door sedans rolled off the line—highest sedan production figure in the 1952–55 era. This year's cost: $3711. 6. Judging by sales figures, the "trend toward Lincoln" wasn't growing quite as quickly as heralded in this ad. Yet, Lincoln rose from 17th to 15th in model-year output.

**1.** These Lincolns are on display at the 1954 Chicago Auto Show. Veteran road-tester Tom McCahill of *Mechanix Illustrated* still considered Lincoln "America's finest and safest automobile." More and brighter colors were offered, on both the Cosmopolitan and costlier Capri series. Under Lincoln hoods, the four-barrel carburetor was improved, hotter spark plugs helped prevent fouling, and a new distributor gave better spark advance control. Brakes grew an inch, to help shorten stopping distances. **2.** Lincoln No. 103 ran second in the stock-car class at the 1954 *Carrera Panamericana* race, driven for the factory by Walt Faulkner. This is a replica of that competitor, complete with appropriate decals. Four factory-backed Lincolns dropped out of the race, but the winner was a privately run Lincoln.

1

2

Final Muntz Jets rolled out of the Illinois plant in 1954, with removable padded hardtops—no soft top at all. Late examples switched from a flathead Lincoln V-8 to the overhead-valve version, and adopted fiberglass fenders.

Big-grilled brainchild of sportsman Sterling Edwards, the $4995 Edwards America rode a Mercury chassis. Two of the six cars built had 205-bhp Lincoln engines; others carried Olds or Cadillac V-8s. High costs precluded volume production.

# 1954 Mercury

1

1. No Mercury beat the $2452 Monterey two-door hardtop in popularity; shoppers picked up 79,533 of them. 2. Four-door sedans came in Custom or Monterey guise, with only an $82 price differential. 3. Value leader was the two-door sedan, offered only as a Custom at $2194. This Merc has stick-shift, but shoppers turned eagerly to Merc-O-Matic. A modest facelift included neatly faired-in wraparound taillights. 4. Like other modern V-8s, the Merc's was over-square—bore larger than stroke. 5. Though festively colored, Mercury's Carnival show car didn't look much different from stock models. 6. The Carnival showed off a red/white interior with uniquely patterned seat and door-panel upholstery.

2

4

3

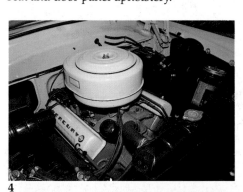

5    6

1. Like Ford's Skyliner, the Monterey Sun Valley had a transparent, green-tinted roof section of quarter-inch Plexiglas. Just 9761 were built, selling for $2582 ($130 more than a plain hardtop). 2. Mercury claimed interior temperatures in a Sun Valley rose only five degrees in direct sunlight, but some disgruntled owners complained of stifling heat. A zip-in vinyl cover kept the sun out completely. Sun Valleys had special interior trim combinations and body color schemes. 3. Dream cars had transparent roofs before, but the Sun Valley and Ford's Skyliner were the first to offer this feature to the public. In addition to making scenery more viewable, the see-through roof was good for overhead traffic lights—and provided the same weather protection as a solid-steel top. 4. Naturally, those who craved full exposure to the elements could select a Monterey convertible for $28 more than a Sun Valley. Ragtops weren't quite as popular, but the plain hardtop coupe beat both by a mile. Engine output took a big leap with introduction of the 256-cid overhead-valve V-8: from a mere 125 horsepower in '53, all the way to 161 bhp.

# 1954 Oldsmobile

1

**1-2.** Oldsmobiles gained new bodyshells, for the biggest change since their 1948-49 redesign. Many declared this year's Olds the best-looking of the decade. Note the flashy two-toning on this Series Ninety-Eight Holiday hardtop. **3.** Series Ninety-Eight Starfire convertibles weren't rare, with 6800 built on a 126-inch wheelbase. Engines were enlarged for the first time, to 324.3 cid. **4.** Oldsmobile touted the show-car origin of its Starfire, with "spectacular sweep-cut" fenders and the "surging might" of its 185-bhp Rocket engine. **5.** Aunt Jemima (of pancake fame) rode in a Starfire convertible for a benefit supper at the factory.

2

4

OLDSMOBILE'S
FABULOUS NEW
*Starfire*

3

5

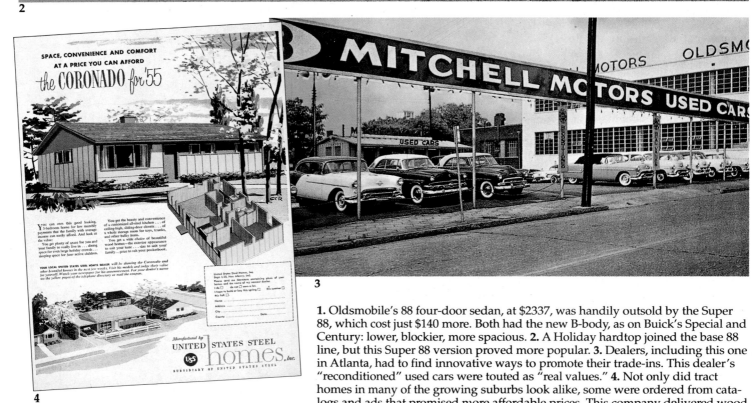

1. Oldsmobile's 88 four-door sedan, at $2337, was handily outsold by the Super 88, which cost just $140 more. Both had the new B-body, as on Buick's Special and Century: lower, blockier, more spacious. 2. A Holiday hardtop joined the base 88 line, but this Super 88 version proved more popular. 3. Dealers, including this one in Atlanta, had to find innovative ways to promote their trade-ins. This dealer's "reconditioned" used cars were touted as "real values." 4. Not only did tract homes in many of the growing suburbs look alike, some were ordered from catalogs and ads that promised more affordable prices. This company delivered wood homes, but some were metal—prefabricated partly or fully.

# 1955 Hudson

## American Motors Corporation

Newly merged company launches crash program to update Nash—and create Nash-based Hudson

Sharing bodyshells and built on same assembly lines, Hudsons are viewed as Nashes in disguise—but differences exist

Full-size Nashes display inboard headlamps; Hudson's sit outboard . . . Hudsons have exposed front wheels, eggcrate grille, and different gauge cluster

AMC offers biggest wraparound windshield in the industry

Hornet continues with 308-cid Championship Six, but Packard V-8 available in Nash and Hudson

Use of Packard V-8 and Twin Ultramatic stems from short-lived step toward possible merger with Studebaker-Packard

Compact Hudson Jet dropped

Ramblers and Metropolitans wear both Nash and Hudson badges

Rambler line consists of a dozen models available in Nash and Hudson showrooms

Ramblers display exposed front wheels and eggcrate grille, and carry 90-horse-power engine

Shipments of Metropolitans to North America plunge nearly 54 percent to 6096 cars

1. Because facelifting the "Step-down" design was virtually impossible, AMC issued Nash-like Hudsons, including this $2460 Custom Wasp sedan. Note the distinctive two-tone paint. 2-3. Custom and Super Wasp sedans made the Hudson line-up. The bold crosshatch grille employed Hudson's familiar triangle badge. Hudsons also had their own taillight design. Wasps borrowed their 202-cid six-cylinder engine from the departed Jet. 4. Both compact (Rambler) and full-size Hudsons shared their basic structures with Nash equivalents, but the two makes differed more than many shoppers believed. 5. Priced only modestly higher than their Nash counterparts, Hudsons included a wealth of equipment, Deep Coil suspension, and big new wraparound windshield.

1. Gaudy colors made a Hudson noticeable, even if its link to Nash displeased some fans. Hornets rode a wheelbase seven inches longer than Wasps. 2. Hornets carried either the familiar 308-cid six (170 horsepower with Twin H-Power) or a 208-bhp, 320-cid V-8 driving Twin Ultramatic. Sedans came in Custom or Super trim. 3. A Wasp Custom Hollywood hardtop cost $2570. 4. Similar in appearance to a Wasp, the longer Hornet Hollywood hardtop went for $2880. 5. Hornets could now have the comfort of All Season air conditioning, the convenience of Airliner reclining seats and travel beds—plus Nash-style unit construction. 6. Fewer families took delivery of a Hudson than in '54, even though most automakers saw their output shoot skyward.

# 1955 Nash

1. A Nash Ambassador Country Club hard-top cost $2795 with six-cylinder power, or $3095 with the new V-8. Pink/white paint might seem frivolous today, but such blends drew customers into the show-rooms. Front wheels again were enclosed, while big Hudsons wore full cutouts.
2. The Ambassador and Statesman stuck with unit construction, claimed "safer, stronger, more rigid." 3. Before she became a successful television actress, Miss America Lee Meriwether graced the cover of Nash's 1955 brochure. 4. Nash ads prof-fered a series of inducements, from roomi-ness and power to durability and comfort, but strong resale value stood high on the list.

Today You've Previewed The Styling Sensation Of The Year

*The New Nash Ambassador And Nash Statesman For 1955*

## NASH NOW TOPS 14 OF ALL 17 MAKES IN RESALE!

1

2

3

**1-2.** Starting price for a Nash Statesman Custom Country Club hardtop was $2495, but this well-loaded example came to $3016. Unique two-toning imparted a four-layer look. The Statesman used Rambler's 195.6-cid six, while Ambassadors had a Clipper V-8 or Nash 252.6-cid six, rated 130 horsepower (140 with dual carburetion). **3.** Nash's Safety-Vu headlights were joined by parking lights at the tips of its forward-thrusting fenders. **4.** Like all big Nashes, the Ambassador Country Club hardtop had a Scena-Ramic wraparound windshield. The 208-bhp Jetfire V-8 came with Twin Ultramatic drive. **5-6.** With the V-8, this Nash Ambassador Custom four-door sedan cost $2965 ($290 more than the six). **7.** More new Nashes than Hudsons were seen on American streets, including this colorful Country Club hardtop.

7

# 1955 Dodge

1

2

3

1. Many called three-toning a fad, but others loved the look of a Dodge Custom Royal Lancer hardtop, here enhanced by fender skirts. "Eyes widen, hearts quicken," said Dodge's sales brochure, "at this dream come true!" Only Custom Royals had small chrome fins atop rear fenders. 2. A Royal Lancer hardtop sold for $2395, with 25,831 built—fewer than the Custom Royal equivalent. 3. More subdued two-toning was used on this Royal four-door sedan, which sold for $2310 and held the mildest V-8 engine, yielding 175 horsepower. 4. Though not quite as plush inside as a Custom Royal, the Dodge Royal's upholstery beckoned enticingly.

4

## CHRYSLER CORPORATION COLORS FOR 1955

 Tango Red (Chrysler)

 Porcelain Green (Chrysler)

 Wisteria Blue (Chrysler)

 Emberglow (DeSoto)

 Cove Green (DeSoto)

 Avon Blue (DeSoto)

 Fantasy Yellow (Dodge)

 Parisian Blue (Dodge)

   Cameo Red (Dodge)

 Chiffon Green (Dodge)

 Pompano Peach (Plymouth)

 Tampa Turquoise (Plymouth)

 Glades Green (Plymouth)

Seminole Scarlet (Plymouth)

1. Now a separate division, Imperial shared its split grille with the Chrysler 300. 2. Famed ventriloquist Edgar Bergen (father of Candice) and Mortimer Snerd—a country cousin of Charlie McCarthy—look pleased with an Imperial Newport. 3. A sedan and hardtop made up the Imperial line. 4. Chrysler shunned subtlety, asserting that an "Imperial bespeaks power, leadership, and good taste." 5. In an Imperial, Chrysler suggested, one expected "glances of approval." 6. "Gunsight" taillights stood free atop Imperial fenders. 7. Exhaust from the 250-bhp V-8 exited from tips in the bumper.

# 1955 Chevrolet

1. Chevrolets featured a Sweep Sight windshield and rakish beltline dip. 2. The twin-cove dashboard design held a central glovebox. 3. License plates still varied in size—as they would until 1957—and color schemes changed from year to year. This Atlas Tire ad also mentioned that dealers were equipped to repair the new tubeless tires. 4. Not many station wagons have achieved near-classic status, but Chevrolet's Nomad is the exception. 5. On November 23, 1954, a gold-trimmed Bel Air hardtop rolled off the line—the 50-millionth car produced by General Motors. 6. GM president Harlow H. Curtice poses with the 50-millionth car, at Flint, Michigan. 7. A Two-Ten Delray coupe cost $1835. 8. A pleated, all-vinyl interior distinguished the Delray, which was based on the two-door sedan.

1

2

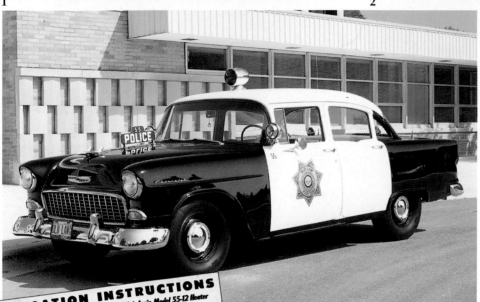

3

New color brilliance
now so easy

with color enriching
DU PONT Nº 7 POLISH

GLOSS METER TEST PROVES IT

DU PONT
AUTO
POLISH
AND CLEANER
Nº 7

4

## INSTALLATION INSTRUCTIONS
For Arvin AC-12 Air Inlet And Defroster Kit For Use With Arvin Model 55-12 Heater
On 1955 Chevrolet Passenger Cars

FOR FASTEST AND EASIEST INSTALLATION FOLLOW THESE STEPS—

A. INSTALL DEFROSTER NOZZLES AND HOSES.
B. MOUNT HEATER TO FIREWALL AS DIRECTED IN FIRST SEVEN STEPS ON "HEATER INSTRUCTION SHEET."
C. FOLLOW INSTRUCTIONS BELOW ON "MOUNTING COWL INLET, FLEXIBLE DUCT, AND BLOWER AIR INLET" BEFORE MOUNTING BLOWER TO FIREWALL.
D. COMPLETE INSTALLATION OF HEATER AS DIRECTED ON HEATER INSTRUCTION SHEET.

5

**1.** Chevrolet's general manager, Thomas H. Keating, piloted the pace car, a Bel Air convertible, for the 39th Indianapolis 500 race. **2.** Speedway board chairman A. C. Hulman directed activity from the pace car. A four-car tangle took the life of leader Bill Vukovich, who'd won the previous two Indy events. **3.** No, this isn't a real police car. It's a converted Chevrolet One-Fifty. **4.** DuPont polish promised to restore "weathered" paint "to new-car brilliance." **5.** An adept do-it-yourselfer could install an aftermarket heater. **6.** Final first-generation Corvettes kept their mesh-covered headlights. **7.** Chevy's sports car could finally boast of V-8 power, but sales totaled less than one-fifth of the '54 tally, at 700. **8.** The Corvette's 265-cid V-8 developed 195 horsepower.

New 195-h.p.
Chevrolet
Corvette
V8

A brilliant new edition
of America's most popular
production sports car

7

6

8

# 1955 Oldsmobile

1

2

3

4

## OLDSMOBILE COLORS FOR 1955

Burlingame Red

Turquoise Iridescent

Twilight Blue

Frost Blue

Chartreuse

Coral

Glen Green Iridescent

Bimini Blue Iridescent

Mist Gray Iridescent

Mint Green

Shell Beige

Regal Maroon

1. Oldsmobiles enjoyed a moderate facelift with "flying-colors" side trim. Like many Ninety-Eight Starfire convertibles, this one is loaded—with Autronic Eye, and power seats and windows. 2. Red/white upholstery gave the Starfire ragtop even greater flair. Note the sharp "dogleg" slant of the windshield pillars. 3. Simoniz gave away a Holiday Ninety-Eight hardtop, plus cash, to the person who wrote the best last line for a limerick about the new Simoniz Easy Method. 4. The Fire Chief of Newark, New Jersey, blazed to the scene in this 88 four-door sedan. At its base price of $2362 (not counting the accessory "gumball" light and fender-mounted bell and siren), the 88 was the only model to came standard with a 185-bhp version of Oldsmobile's 324.3-cid V-8.

1. With 202 horses on tap, an Oldsmobile Super 88 convertible could be hard to catch. Its engine also was optional in regular 88 Olds models. 2. Slipping into an open Super 88 still produced shivers in young Americans—but many began to shun Oldsmobiles in favor of Power-Packed Chevrolets and Fords. 3. *Motor Trend* called the 88s "family hot rods." 4. Oldsmobile's Holiday hardtop sedan arrived at midyear in all three series. Shown is a Super 88. 5. Unlike some long-lived food services, Denny's coffee shops don't look all that different today from their appearance in the mid-1950s.

# Studebaker-Packard Corporation

Packards get heavy facelift with wraparound windshield on same basic bodyshell as '51 models

V-8 engines go into Packards

Packard fields three series: Clipper, Clipper Custom, and trio of big Packard models

Tech-oriented Packards feature Torsion-Level ride with motor-controlled torsion bars instead of the customary springs

Limited-production Caribbeans wear three-tone paint treatment

Packard's new Twin Ultramatic starts in Low, locks out at cruising speed—proves to be an unreliable transmission

Packard produces 55,247 cars for 14th place—up from 16th . . . lower-cost Clippers account for bulk of sales

Top-line President series, a name not used since 1942, replaces Studebaker Land Cruiser sedan; four models offered

Studebaker Speedster features wild two-tone paint, quilted-vinyl interior, tooled dashboard

Studebaker builds 116,333 cars for 12th place (up from 13th)

January sees start of 36-day strike

Studebaker-Packard firm reports profit in first quarter, but suffers $30 million net loss in first full year of operation

1

2

3

4

Head of its Class
in Everything....

**QUALITY** *The look will convince you the 1955 Clipper stands at the head of its class. Built by Packard Craftsmen to the highest standards in the industry. Seen is luxury and quality at a medium price.*

**SIZE** *Roomy fit best of glamorous exterior styling affords extra head room, shoulder room, leg room and leg room . . . more room throughout for truly royal comfort.*

**POWER** *Clipper V-8 engines deliver 245 and 225 horsepower . . . more driving force in the rear wheels of all road speeds. Here any other car in its field. And instead with these engines is Packard's new Twin Ultramatic Transmission . . . smooth as its iron in give you lingertip choice of lightning getaway or smoothest cruising glide.*

*See and drive the 1955 Clipper . . . a product of Packard Division, Studebaker-Packard Corporation.*

***Visit Your Packard Dealer . . . Take The Key and See.***

*For Those Who Desire Individuality*

The 1955 *Clipper*

Built by Packard Craftsmen

5

**1-2.** Packard Clipper Customs, including this $3076 Constellation hardtop, got a 245-horsepower version of the new 352-cid engine. Basic Clippers used a 225-bhp, 320-cid V-8. Accessories included a four-way power seat and Wonderbar radio. For their final serious stab at the market, Packards had to be fresh and innovative—and they were, with major advances in styling, engineering, and marketing. **3.** Even apart from the hood script, the ship's wheel grille insignia reveals that this Packard is a Clipper—either Custom or basic. **4.** Packard's intense redesign didn't overlook the interior, which featured glittery gauges and a central glovebox. **5.** An ornate grille and "cathedral" taillights, hurriedly penned by Richard Teague, marked the big Packards, but lower-cost Clippers had 1954-style taillights and their own grille design.

1. The 352-cid V-8 in the $5932 Packard Caribbean was rated at 275 horsepower. Senior Packards' wheelbase remained 127 inches. 2. Tri-toning could also be ordered on a Four Hundred, which was priced $2000 below the Caribbean. 3. Ads boasted of Packard's new Torsion-Level suspension. 4. In a Four Hundred, the V-8 yielded 260 bhp. 5. More than 7200 Four Hundred hardtops were built. 6. Design chief Bill Schmidt studies Teague's taillight rendering. 7. Exhaust gases exited via neat outlets at the bumper tips. 8. Every detail on the Four Hundred clamored for attention.

251

# 1956 Hudson

## American Motors Corporation

Rambler earns complete redesign, wears Hudson or Nash badge

All Ramblers have four doors on 108-inch wheelbase

Rambler Cross Country debuts as the first four-door hardtop station wagon

Ramblers come in seven models and three trim levels (DeLuxe, Super, Custom); AMC pushes harder on "compact" designation

Rambler's engine is transformed from L-head to overhead-valve

Full-size models are facelifted, as AMC makes stronger effort to separate Nash and Hudson makes

Hudsons earn jeers for overblown styling; equivalent Nash models look somewhat more restrained

AMC-built V-8 replaces Packard engine in Hudson Hornet and Nash Ambassador at mid-season

Hudson Hornet Special arrives at midyear on Wasp chassis; Nash Ambassador also gets Special

Metropolitans get mid-season facelift and bigger engine

Rambler sets transcontinental economy record at 32.09 mpg—costs less than a penny a mile

Hudson again ranks 15th in production; Nash sinks to 12th

1

2

66 [AMC] has made itself not only lean and hard, but rock-hard during its reorganization of the past two years. The American Motors program has concentrated the facilities of two companies—Nash and Hudson—into a tightly integrated operation, with probably the lowest break-even point in the industry. 99

*American Motors president* **George Romney**; *October 1956*

1-2. With Twin H-Power, the six-cylinder engine in a Hudson Hornet Custom four-door sedan produced 175 horsepower. A Continental-style outside spare remained available on full-size models. Styled by consultant Richard Arbib, the '56 Hudsons were viewed by many as excessive—or even bizarre, bordering on the grotesque.
3. In March, the Clipper V-8 (borrowed from Packard) was replaced by AMC's own V-8 engine: 250 cid and 190 horsepower, with new Flashaway Hydra-Matic optional. Compared to its 320-cid predecessor, though, the new motor lacked "go" power.

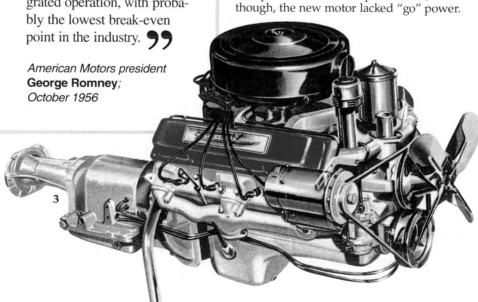

3

1

2

3

THE **BIG** CAR WITH **BIG** CHANGES IS THE STYLE SENSATION OF '56

1956 Hornet has new Safety-Torque V-8 power... smart, new V-Line styling... 3 times softer, smoother ride

**Hudson Hornet V-8**
The most beautiful performer of them all!

5

4

**1-2.** Hardtops never were a high-volume item at Hudson, so only 1640 Hornet Hollywoods were built this season. The huge eggcrate grille was interrupted by a "V" carrying the Hudson emblem at the top, dipping in another V-shape at the bottom. A small chrome fin topped each taillight. **3.** Designed in-house, Hudson's instrument cluster looked relatively plain for this gaudy period—especially when compared to the garish body. **4.** Ramblers had an all-new shape for 1956, as ads asked: "Why be satisfied with the 'All Three Look'?" Except for badging, a Hudson Rambler looked the same as a Nash version, featuring a box-section Fashion Safety Arch over the rear window. The four-door Custom Cross Country wagon cost $2329, but a Super wagon could be purchased for $96 less. Three-tone paint cost extra. Hydra-Matic was popular on top Ramblers. **5.** "V-Line" styling failed to send Hudson into the high-sales arena. Hudson promised a ride that was "3 times softer, smoother."

1

3

1. Imperial wheelbases grew three inches. This luminous sedan has extra-cost wire wheels. 2. A rear-fender tip rotated to reveal an Imperial's gas filler. Mild but sweeping fins held "gunsight" lights. 3. Chances are, these newlyweds had more on their minds than Flying A's Ethyl gasoline. Ethyl additive turned fuel from regular into high-octane. 4. A row of round gauges and knobs dominated the dashboard of an Imperial Southampton. 5. Roll down the back window of an Imperial Southampton and the adjoining vent wing lowered at the same time. 6. The Imperial line expanded to include both two- and four-door Southampton hardtops.

2

4

5

6

1. Ghia, of Italy, did the bodywork for Crown Imperial sedans and limousines. Only 226 were built this year. 2. Crown Imperial limos had a rear jump seat for eight-passenger capacity. 3. Both Crown Imperial models rode an extended (149.5-inch) wheelbase. 4. Government dignitaries could parade in a specially built Imperial convertible sedan—a body style that never reached regular production. 5. There's some confusion as to whether the Norseman was to be a concept car or merely a test bed for its unique cantilevered roof, which was supported only by the rear pillars. In the end, it was neither; the Norseman was being transported from Italian builder Ghia aboard the *Andrea Doria* when the ship sank in July of 1956.

267

# 1956 Continental

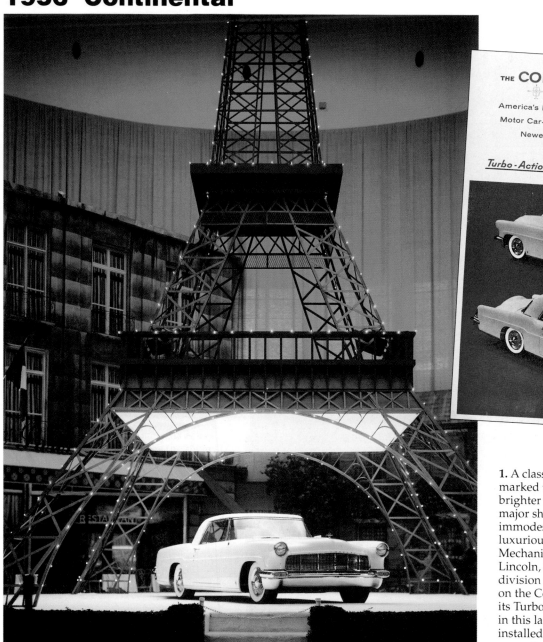

1. A classic long-hood/short-deck profile marked the Continental Mark II—Ford's brighter idea, attempting to recapture a major share of the high-end market. Their immodest goal: to create America's most luxurious, carefully crafted production car. Mechanical components were shared with Lincoln, but Continental began as a Ford division unto itself. 2. Champion jumped on the Continental bandwagon, noting that its Turbo-Action spark plugs were installed in this latest luxury machine. 3. Tacky if installed on a lesser car, the simulated spare-tire bulge looked just right on a Continental coupe—reminiscent of 1940–48 ancestors.

1

2

**1.** Continental Mark II bodies demanded 60 hours for metal finishing alone—five times the effort on a "normal" automobile. Drivetrain components were machined to high tolerances. The 368-cid V-8 sent 285 horsepower to Turbo-Drive automatic. **2.** Interiors were fitted with old-fashioned broadcloth and nylon, or fine leather could be ordered. Round gauges included a tachometer and chronometer. A "cowbelly" frame resulted in a recessed floor, not unlike the old "Step-down" Hudsons. Each chassis was tuned and tested before mounting the body. **3.** Understated elegance was the byword, promising a lasting "experience" rather than a mere adventure. To help attain "ride control," Continentals had temperature-sensitive shock absorbers. **4.** After exhaustive testing and inspection, Continentals were shipped in a fleece-lined cloth cover—wrapped in a plastic bag.

3

4

# 1956 Mercury

1. At the low end of Mercury's range, a Medalist hardtop coupe cost $2398. Early models lacked part of the "lightning bolt" side trim. 2. Most popular Mercury was the $2765 Montclair hardtop coupe. 3. Mercury dubbed its Montclair four-door hardtop a "Phaeton," borrowing a name from prewar days to identify convertible sedans. 4. All hardtops adopted the Montclair's roofline (shown). Each Merc held a 312-cid V-8. 5. In many states, turning sixteen meant you could get a driver's license—and haul over to the local Dairy Queen for those soft-frozen sundaes.

It's Sweet Sixteen for DAIRY QUEEN

16¢ SPECIAL VALUE
STRAWBERRY SUNDAE
JUNE 16th

HOMOGENIZED AND PASTEURIZED
DAIRY QUEEN

16th Birthday SALE

DAIRY QUEEN

Over 3,000 Dairy Queen Stores to Serve You!

NATIONAL DAIRY QUEEN DEVELOPMENT CO.
800 Safe Bldg., Davenport, Iowa

1

1. Carousel Red paint on this Mercury Custom convertible was "flo-toned" with Classic White to emulate Montclair trim. 2. Monterey stood just below Montclair in Mercury's hierarchy. This $2555 sedan sold better than mates in other series. 3. Six- and eight-passenger wagons came in Custom (shown) and Monterey form. 4. A two-door Custom started at $2351. 5. The experimental XM-Turnpike Cruiser debuted at the Chicago Auto Show, "designed to take full advantage of the nation's budding new improved highway system." Transparent "butterfly" roof inserts lifted as doors opened. Concave channels ended in huge vee'd taillights.

2

3

4

5

# 1956 Buick

## General Motors Corporation

Four-door Cadillac, Chevrolet, and Pontiac hardtops debut

Mildly facelifted Buick stays in third place in industry

Improved Buick Dynaflow runs with two stator wheels

All Buicks, including Special series, have 322-cid V-8

Cadillac engine is bored to 365 cid—285 or 305 horsepower

Cadillac Eldorado buyers get two posh choices: Biarritz convertible or Seville hardtop

Unlike most makes, Cadillac enjoys increase in model-year output—up nearly 10 percent

Chevrolet earns modest restyle and stronger engine selection

Corvettes get "second generation" restyling

Oldsmobile engines gain power . . . Pontiac's V-8 is bored to 316.6 cubic inches

Lightweight Pontiac Chieftain two-door sedan with 285-bhp engine sets world record, traveling 2841 miles in 24 hours

A Pontiac beats all Eights in the Mobilgas Economy Run

Alfred P. Sloan steps down as GM's chairman in April

Semon E. "Bunkie" Knudsen, Pontiac's new general manager, vows to beat Olds in sales

1

GREAT NEW SOURCE OF POWER for your car!

Only Texaco **Sky Chief** gasoline is supercharged with **PETROX**... the exclusive petroleum-base element... to keep your engine younger longer, to give you all the knock-free power your engine can deliver... and greater gasoline mileage.

Only Texaco Sky Chief gives you 1 · 2 · 3 power!

**1** PETROX...

**2** TOP OCTANE...

**3** 100% CLIMATE-CONTROLLED...

TEXACO DEALERS
IN ALL 48 STATES

3

2

1. Front sheetmetal for Buicks was new, with a vee'd grille and teardrop-shaped Ventiports. All models now had rounded rear wheel wells. The Riviera name was used solely for hardtops—both two-door and the new four-door, offered in each of the four series. 2. Roadmaster (shown) and Super four-door sedans were six-window designs, while Special and Century had a four-window profile. 3. Then, as now, oil companies concocted impressive claims for their products, and fancy names for additives—like the protective Petrox that went into Sky Chief gasoline. Increasingly powerful V-8s demanded more from fuels. Unless octane ratings kept pace, engine knock could be a problem as compression ratios approached 10:1.

1

2

3

4

5

6

7

8

**1.** Each Buick series had a convertible. Wire wheels added dash—and dollars—to a radiant Roadmaster. Specials got a 220-bhp engine; others, a 255-bhp version of the 322-cid V-8. **2.** Of Buick's 21,676 ragtops, 22 percent wore a Century badge. **3.** A Century Riviera hardtop cost $343 less than the convertible. **4.** Just $2457 bought a Special Riviera hardtop—the top-selling Buick. **5.** A $3256 Century Estate wagon flaunted its three-toning. **6.** Only the Special series included both two- and four-door pillared sedans. **7.** Station wagon bodies get final attention at Ionia Manufacturing Company—GM's only outside body supplier. **8.** Buick's fiberglass-bodied Centurion appeared at the GM Motorama. A TV camera substituted for the rearview mirror. **9.** "Big Bill" Gardner claimed to have a used car "corral" in every corner of Milwaukee, Wisconsin.

9

# 1956 Studebaker

1

2

**1.** Studebaker Presidents shifted to a shorter wheelbase, except for the fancy new Classic sedan—priced $254 above an ordinary President four-door. Designers sought a more massive look for the sedans and wagons, resulting in a squared-off profile and large mesh grille, which helped disguise the carryover bodyshell. Studebaker-Packard's financial woes precluded a major redesign at this time. **2.** Each President model carried a 289-cid V-8, rated 195, 210, or 225 horsepower. Studebakers might have a conventional column three-speed, overdrive, or Flight-O-Matic. **3.** Only the President Classic sedan (shown) and the Hawk coupes rode a 120.5-inch wheelbase. Meanwhile, low-budget two-door sedanets joined the Champion and Commander series. Studebaker issued more than 85,400 cars in the '56 model year, including 19,165 Hawks.

3

1. Each Studebaker series had a station wagon, topped by the $2529 President Pinehurst. Note the oddly patterned two-toning. 2. Four small round gauges sat in a panel ahead of the driver of a sedan or wagon. Optional air conditioning went below the dashboard. 3. Studebaker prices ranged from $1844 to $2529—similar to Chevrolet's. 4. A Pinehurst's 289-cid V-8 made 195 or 225 horsepower.

Can this be a low price car?

Yes! Studebaker has brought *Craftsmanship* with a *Flair* to the low price field . . . that's why it's the big new choice among low price cars!

The big new choice in the low price field—**Studebaker**

# 1957 Hudson

## American Motors Corporation

Nash and Hudson names used for last time, as full-size models face final season in lineup

Nash Ambassador gets rather extensive restyling; Hudson Hornet changes less

Full-size cars hold new 327-cid V-8 engine

Ramblers gain mild facelift, can have V-8 engine for first time

Rambler is now a separate make, with no Nash or Hudson badge

Super-swift Rambler Rebel four-door hardtop arrives at midyear, powered by 327-cid V-8

Fuel injection is planned for Rebel, but no production models are so equipped . . . was to be "the compact car with LIGHTNING under the hood"

Overdrive-equipped Rambler Cross Country wagon goes on coast-to-coast economy run—gets 32.09 mpg, consuming only five tankfuls

By year-end, Metropolitans wear their own badges; sales pick up sharply, to 15,317 cars (13,425 for U.S., the rest to Canada)

President George Romney orders big cars dropped at midyear, after only 3876 Hudson Hornets and 3561 Nash Ambassadors are built; company will focus on Ramblers

1

2

3

> **66** This is legally and economically absurd. **99**
>
> *American Motors president* **George Romney**, *on the disparity between restrictions on auto prices and theoretically unlimited wages for auto workers; March 1957*

**1-2.** Mild trim shuffling improved the look of final Hudsons, but they still ranked as garish. Wasps were gone, leaving only a Hornet sedan and hardtop. **3.** Tacked-on tailfins were body-colored. **4.** Three-tone paint remained common on Hornets, including this Hollywood hardtop. All Hudsons had a 255-horsepower, 327-cid V-8.

4

1

2

3

4

**1-2.** A relatively radical facelift graced the big Nashes. The Statesman departed, leaving only Ambassadors, like this $2847 Custom Country Club hardtop. **3-4.** Headlights returned to the fenders, and Nash was one of the first makes with standard dual lights (except where the four-headlight setup remained illegal). Front wheels were fully exposed for the first time since 1948. Enlarged to 327 cid, the V-8 made 255 bhp.

# 1957 Nash

1

2

3

4

**1.** Custom Ambassadors wore extra side trim for three-toning, and featured posher interiors. **2.** AMC gambled its future on the proposition that Americans didn't want a "big, over-chromiumed rolling cabana" but would accept a frugal car if it were sufficiently roomy. **3-4.** To demonstrate its reliance upon Rambler for the future, AMC launched the Rebel. This limited-edition four-door hardtop held AMC's four-barrel 255-horsepower V-8 engine—borrowed from the big cars. That was sufficient to propel a Rebel to 60 mph in as little as 7.2 seconds. Painted light silver metallic, Rebels had a gold anodized aluminum sidespear.

1

**1-2.** Altered only in detail, a Rambler Custom Cross Country station wagon cost $2500. The 195.6-cid six-cylinder engine got a boost to 125 horsepower (135-bhp optional). On Custom models, the upper bodyside chrome strip ran straight back to the taillights. The new 250-cid, 190-horsepower V-8 engine option included dual exhausts. **3.** Little-changed and no longer badged as Nash or Hudson, a Metropolitan hardtop cost $1567. **4.** The Metro convertible ran $24 more than a hardtop. Both retained the little rear-mounted spare tire, and typically sported colorful two-toning.

2

❝There's a certain romance for people in buying a car imported from Europe.❞

*American Motors automotive distribution vice-president* **Roy Abernethy**, *on the success of AMC's imported Metropolitan, and other European automobiles; March 1957*

4

3

# Chrysler Corporation

All Chrysler products feature Virgil Exner's second-generation "Forward Look"

Exner, known for stunning show cars, spends $300 million for this year's redesign

Each make is long, low, sleek—with soaring, flamboyant fins

Torsion-bar suspensions replace conventional front springs on all Chrysler Corporation cars

Three-speed TorqueFlite automatic transmission, introduced on '56 Imperials, is available on all makes

Most V-8 engines gain in displacement and power, following industry trend

Rear-facing seats available in station wagons . . . transistor radios are installed . . . cars ride new 14-inch wheels

Chrysler offers four models: Windsor, Saratoga, New Yorker, and bold 300-C, the last adding a convertible

DeSoto adds lower-cost Firesweep series and open Adventurer

Imperials get a bodyshell of their own and display curved side window glass

Plymouth returns to Number Three ranking for first time since '54, ahead of Buick and Oldsmobile by a wide margin

Chrysler products suffer rattles, leaks, premature rust

1

3

2

66 At the moment, we are embarrassed—and seriously—by a shortage of automobiles. 99

*Chrysler Corporation president* **L. L. "Tex" Colbert,** *on Chrysler's inability to meet dealer demand for the all-new 1957 models; December 1956*

1. A broadened Chrysler lineup brought back the Saratoga as middle member, between the Windsor and New Yorker. Each rode a 126-inch wheelbase, including this skirted New Yorker two-door hardtop, which started at $4202. A total of 8863 were built. 2. Fins soared tall on New Yorkers and all Chrysler products, part of the "Forward Look" that helped the company grab styling leadership from GM. 3. With 10,948 built, Chrysler's $4259 New Yorker four-door hardtop outsold the two-door version. Output slipped a bit, but Chrysler stayed in 10th place, behind the perennial luxury favorite—Cadillac.

1

2

3

1. Chrysler New Yorkers wore the new look particularly well. New Torsion-Aire suspension aimed to boost handling, not just ride quality. 2. Windsor convertibles were dropped, but the New Yorker ragtop carried on with a 325-horsepower rendition of the 392-cid Hemi V-8. This example has Highway Hi-Fi. Just 1049 were built. 3. At the supercar level, a 300-C convertible joined the hardtop coupe.

> 66 You can look for it in body panels, bumpers, more aluminum roofs, fender panels, decklids, and hoods. 99
>
> **Reynolds Metals Company spokesman**, *on future automotive applications of aluminum; March 1957*

# 1957 Chrysler

1

2

3

1. Chrysler's 300-C had a distinct grille for the first time. Its Hemi grew to 392 cid and 375 or 390 bhp. 2. A round badge identified the 300-C, colored to suggest its U.S. origin. 3. A 300-C convertible cost $5359. Five colors were available, all monotones, with minimal trim. Manual shift now was available, but seldom ordered. 4. Chrysler called the 300-C "America's greatest performing car," proven by speed runs at Daytona. A total of 2402 were built, 484 of them convertibles.

66 The board wishes to encourage owners and drivers to evaluate passenger cars in terms of useful power and ability to afford safe, reliable, and comfortable transportation, rather than in terms of capacity for speed. 99

*Official statement of the board of directors, **Automobile Manufacturers Assn.**, on its decision to impose a racing ban on member companies; June 1957*

4

1

2

4

3

1-2. DeSoto's Adventurer became a two-model series, as a convertible joined the hardtop. This one holds a Highway Hi-Fi record player and Benrus steering wheel watch. Breathing through twin four-barrel carburetors, the Hemi V-8 engine now measured 345 cid and yielded 345 horses—one per cubic inch. Only 300 convertibles were built, priced at $4272. 3-4. An Adventurer hardtop went for $3997, with 1650 produced. Torsion-Aire suspension helped reduce tilt and sway in hard cornering, and also eased the ride.

# 1957 Imperial

1. An expanded lineup included the Imperial, Imperial Crown, and Imperial LeBaron. Hardtop sedans came in each series, and a gorgeous Crown convertible debuted. 2. Imperial wheelbases shrank to 129 inches. The V-8 engine now measured 392 cid and 325 horsepower—again shared with New Yorkers. Torsion-Aire front suspension gave Imperials a strong selling point. 3. Texaco had quite a list of maintenance steps for dealer service shops—22 shown here, from checking ignition points to adjusting belts. Then as now, service work helped the dealer's bottom line, so it was essential to convince customers that each mechanic was a "trained specialist" and "the best friend your car has ever had." 4. Movie/TV cowboy Roy Rogers waves from behind the wheel of a four-door Imperial.

1

2

3

**1.** Again painted off-white and gold, Plymouth's $2925 Fury hardtop got a brand-new engine—biggest in the low-priced field. Production rose to 7438 cars. More than three inches lower and four inches wider, with the industry's lowest beltline and towering "shark" fins out back, Plymouths ranked among the best looking '57 cars. They appeared to be longer than ever, but actually measured slightly shorter overall. **2.** Plymouth wheelbases, including Fury's, grew to 118 inches (122 inches for wagons). **3.** Even the air-cleaner housings were gold-colored on the new V-800 dual-quad 318-cid Fury engine, which developed 290 horsepower and 325 pound-feet of torque, running on 9.25:1 compression. The engine was optional in any Plymouth model. Dealer-installed safety belts were available, but not widely advertised.

# 1957 Plymouth

1

SUDDENLY, IT'S 1960...PLYMOUTH!

In one flaming moment, Plymouth leaps three full years ahead—the only car that dares to break the time barrier! Plymouth's traditionally great engineering brings you tremendous power for safety with the fabulous new Fury "301" V-8 engine...revolutionary new Torsion-Aire ride...exhilarating new sports car handling...new super-safe Total Contact Brakes...dramatic Flight-Sweep Styling. The car you might have expected in 1960 is at your dealer's now! See it!...Drive it!...Buy it!

3

2

4

**1-2.** A Plymouth Belvedere sport sedan (four-door hardtop) sold for $2419.
**3.** Plymouth wasn't so far off the mark in claiming that its '57 models were three years ahead of their time. A new Fury 301-cid V-8 yielded 215 horsepower (235 with PowerPak), promising "tremendous power for safety." **4.** Close to 10,000 Belvedere convertibles were built, at $2638. **5.** Gauges sat in a large upright pod on the low-profile dashboard, which held the mirror. Five buttons operated the TorqueFlite transmission. **6.** A mid-level Savoy two-door went for just $2147.

6

5

310

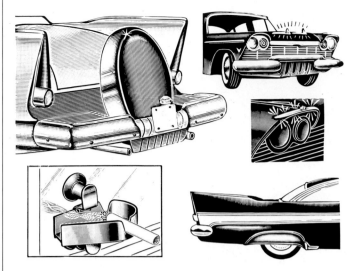

1. Dealers still had to push hard to move cars, despite all the flamboyant styling touches. At Plymouth and every other manufacturer, interior fabric choices were assuming crucial importance.  **2.** Plymouth owners had a long list of aftermarket accessories to choose from in the J. C. Whitney catalog, including a Continental kit, double hood ornament, headlight trim, fender skirts, and handy suction-cup ashtray. **3.** Plymouth's new 318-cid V-800 engine was destined to see long life. Torsion-Aire Ride dispensed with customary coil springs in favor of long front torsion bars. In Plaza models, the Hy-Fire 277-cid V-8 delivered 197 horsepower, while the L-head six got a hike to 132 bhp.  **4.** Could Plymouth have issued a Belvedere four-door convertible? This designer's rendering looks workable and tempting, at least in theory.

# 1957 Ford

# Ford Motor Company

Fords show sculptured-look restyle—Fairlane trim is inspired by Mystere show car

Four Ford series go on sale: Custom, Custom 300, Fairlane, and posh Fairlane 500

Ford Skyliner coupe has retractable steel hardtop

Fords come on 116- or 118-inch wheelbase, with choice of five V-8s or six-cylinder engine

Ford launches Ranchero car-pickup—first such body style since World War II

Supercharged 312-cid Thunderbird V-8 thunders out as much as 340 horsepower

Ford outsells Chevrolet for model year, with record 1.67 million cars built

Lincoln fields Premiere and cheaper Capri series, including new Landau four-door hardtop

Lincoln's V-8 now develops 300 horsepower and 415 pound-feet of torque

Output drops to 41,123, but Lincoln clings to 14th place

Mercury gets its own body structure, with distinctive concave rear panels . . . wheelbases stretch to 122 inches, bodies are lower by four inches

Gadget-laden Mercury Turnpike Cruiser features retractable, reverse-slanted back window and 49-position driver's seat

1

2

3

4

1. New from the ground up and four inches lower than before, Fords borrowed many styling touches from the Mystere show car. Not since 1949 had so much change occurred. This brightly-hued Fairlane 500 Sunliner cost $2505. 2. Shoppers selected a fabric-topped convertible over the new Skyliner coupe by nearly a 4-to-1 margin. 3. First production car with a retractable steel top was Ford's Fairlane 500 Skyliner. In this complex system, the roof's forward section tucked under so it would fit into the trunk area. Despite a hefty price (starting at $2942), 20,766 Skyliners were built this year. 4. Tie-in ads promoted both Fords and vacation destinations. Ford's V-8 engine marked its 25th anniversary in 1957.

1

1. Slowest-selling Fairlane was the Victoria hardtop sedan. 2. In the plush Fairlane 500 series, four-door hardtops were outsold by two-door mates. 3. Because of new thin-pillar styling, the Fairlane 500 club sedan looked almost like a hardtop. 4. A new Custom 300 sedan series replaced the Customline. 5. Lowest-cost Fords were in the Custom series. This practical Tudor sedan cost $1991. 6. Automakers tested cars in extreme temperatures, as evidenced by this frozen Ford wagon. 7. J. C. Whitney catalogs tempted Ford owners with an outside spare tire, wheel covers, and a conversion kit for the new quad headlights.

2

> 66 It's a husky youngster, and like most other new parents, we are proud enough to pop our buttons. 99
>
> *Ford Motor Co. chairman* **Ernest R. Breech**, *on the new Edsel; August 1957*

3

7

6

4

5

# General Motors Corporation

Oldsmobile marks its 60th anniversary; all 88s add "Golden Rocket" nomenclature

Buicks earn ambitious restyle and bigger V-8 engine

Reworked Cadillac is inspired by Eldorado Brougham and Park Avenue show cars

Fuel-injected V-8 engines optional in Chevrolet, Pontiac

Restyled Chevrolet lags Ford in production, but will become far more prized as time goes by

Chevrolet's V-8 grows to 283 cid, developing up to one horsepower per cubic inch (with fuel injection)

Fuel-injected Corvette can do 0–60 mph in just 5.7 seconds

Heavy-duty racing suspension available for Corvettes

Three-speed triple-turbine Turboglide, with hill retarder, is available in Chevrolets

Station wagons return to Oldsmobile lineup

Triple-carburetor J-2 option gives Oldsmobiles 300 horsepower

Fast, flashy Pontiac Bonneville comes with fuel-injected V-8

Tri-Power (three-carburetor) engines available in Pontiacs, mainly for stock-car racing

Pillared sedans depart from Cadillac line

1

2

3

1. Though all-new in structure, Buick's restyling was evolutionary. Roadmasters now came in two series: 70 and an upmarket 75 (shown), with custom interiors and scads of extras. This hardtop sedan cost $4483. 2. Only 2065 folks got their hands on a $3981 Super convertible. All Buicks got a bored/stroked 364-cid V-8, yielding 300 horsepower in all models except the Special. 3. Top executives met at the GM styling studios in the Technical Center: (*from left*) chairman Albert Bradley, former president C. E. Wilson, president Harlow H. Curtice, and design chief Harley J. Earl. GM promoted the close tie between company officers and the styling staff.

*Buick—*
*No.1 on the Zest-seller list*

**Big Thrill's Buick**

> We are testing these cars under the toughest conditions in the world insofar as brakes are concerned.

*Buick chief engineer Verner P. Mathews, on Buick's 196-mile brake-test course on streets in and around Los Angeles; April 1957*

**1.** This gracious home welcomes a pair of Buicks, led by a Super Riviera four-door hardtop. **2.** Most popular Century was the hardtop sedan. Despite added weight, this year's Century was the fastest yet. **3.** Two-door Century hardtops sold slower than their four-door cousins. **4.** New this year was the Century Caballero station wagon, a four-door hardtop style. **5.** Ads continued to suggest an experience akin to aircraft, referring to Buick's "flight deck of a hood." **6.** This Super convertible shows off its two-tone interior, padded dash, and diamond-tooled instrument panel.

# 1957 Cadillac

1

2

3

4  5

❝ We have been selling about as many cars as all our luxury competitors combined. ❞

*Cadillac general manager* **James M. Roche**, *on the marque's successful 1957 model year; September 1957*

**1-2.** Super-luxury shoppers had a new choice: Cadillac's Eldorado Brougham hardtop sedan. Only 400 were virtually hand-built, with air suspension, a stainless-steel roof—and a whopping $13,074 price tag. Note the rear-hinged back doors. **3.** Eldorados earned a full restyling with inboard, sharply pointed fins. Cadillac issued 1800 Biarritz convertibles. **4.** An Eldorado Seville hardtop cost exactly the same ($7286) as an open Biarritz. **5.** Dual carburetion boosted the Eldo's V-8 to 325 horsepower, versus 300 for ordinary Cadillacs.

5

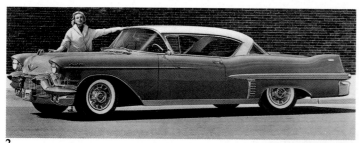

1

2

3

4

> We were told by the Russians that the average American workman is starving. They said only executives and supervisors could own cars and homes. Now we write our relatives and friends and tell them how wrong the Russians were.

**Unidentified Hungarian refugee**, *one of several hired as trainee mechanics at Cadillac's Detroit factory; January 1957*

5

**1.** All Cadillac Series 62 sedans were now pillarless. A base hardtop (shown) cost $4781, versus $5256 for the plusher Sedan de Ville. A new tubular-center X-member chassis enhanced rigidity. **2.** Coupe de Villes sold almost as well as the less-costly Series 62 hardtop. Cadillacs sat two inches lower, with forward-slanting A-pillars and reworked fins. **3.** Now hardtop-styled, the plush Fleetwood Sixty Special sedan continued to sell well, with 24,000 produced. **4.** Series 75 limos cost $7678, but an eight-passenger sedan went for $238 less. Note how doors are cut into the roof. **5.** Marilyn Monroe waves from a Cadillac convertible to open a soccer game at Ebbets Field in Brooklyn, New York.

# 1957 Chevrolet

1

1. If any car defines the Fifties, it has to be the amply facelifted '57 Chevy. Chevrolet issued 166,426 Bel Air sport coupes, typically loaded with extra-cost goodies.  2. The sport sedan never held quite the allure of its two-door sibling, especially as a Two-Ten. Seven engine choices ranged from the 140-horsepower six all the way to a fuel-injected 283-cid V-8, cranking out as much as 283 horsepower.  3. Turquoise was an enticing color choice for a Bel Air convertible. A total of 47,562 were built, starting at $2511.  4. Detroit industrialist Ruben Allender produced a handful of El Moroccos in 1956-57, with Cadillac-like styling touches built around a Chevrolet body and chassis. Taking the Eldorado Brougham as a guide, R. Allender & Co. issued hardtops as well as convertibles, priced less than $500 above a stock Bel Air. Under the hood sat the 220-bhp version of Chevrolet's 283-cid V-8, and a Powerglide transmission.  5. DuPont wax doubtlessly helped bring out the lustrous sheen of some of those turquoise ragtops.

2

3

"I did a clean-and-wax job in 55 minutes

with Du Pont's NEW CAR WAX

...6 months later it's still mirror-bright"

says George T. Duffin of Los Altos, Calif., after waxing his '57 Chevrolet with Du Pont New Car Wax. George found that this new paste wax is as easy to use as a liquid polish, because it cleans, waxes and glazes—all in one easy application. And it protects with real Carnauba wax, the toughest wax known. Proof of protection is the long-lasting gleam. Six months, 11 car washings later, the finish still shows clear reflections of George and his wife! Try Du Pont New Car Wax—it makes any finish look new. At service stations and auto supply stores. Only $2.00.

NEW CAR WAX

DUPONT  BETTER THINGS FOR BETTER LIVING ... THROUGH CHEMISTRY

5

4

1

2

3

**Drive it as your own!** (Get the Hertz Idea)

Yes, drive it as your own—a day, week or longer. That courteous young lady in the Hertz cap will give you the keys to the car you like to drive—a shining, new Powerglide Chevrolet Bel Air or other fine car! You'll save time on business or vacation trips. How? By leaving your car at home, traveling faster by plane or train, then renting a Hertz car there. All you do is show your driver's license and proper identification. Cost? The low national average rate is only $8.00 a day plus 8 cents a mile (down by the week). That includes all gasoline, oil and proper insurance. In addition to the Hertz charge card, we also honor air, Diners' Club and most all hotel credit cards, for your own traveling convenience.

That's The Hertz Idea. To be sure of a car at your destination—anywhere—make a reservation in advance by calling your local Hertz office. We're listed under "Hertz" in alphabetical phone books everywhere! Hertz Rent A Car, 218 South Wabash Avenue, Chicago 4, Illinois.

**More people by far... use HERTZ Rent a car**

Hertz—largest and finest rent a car service—rents the cars you like to drive—Chevrolets and other fine cars!

4

5

6

7

8

9

10

1. Another 6103 Nomad wagons went on sale before Chevy killed this exciting body style. **2.** For every Nomad, more than four times as many Bel Air Townsman four-door wagons were built. **3.** Best-selling Bel Air was a practical pillared four-door sedan. **4.** Millions of drivers had never rented a car, but Hertz had Chevrolets waiting. **5.** Any Chevrolet might be fuel-injected, but the $484 tariff helped limit sales. **6.** With Ramjet injection and 10.5:1 compression, the top V-8 made 283 bhp. **7.** Who'd have guessed that this bland One-Fifty utility sedan held a fuelie? **8.** Corvette output almost doubled, to 6339 cars. **9.** Corvettes could have a 250- or 283-bhp fuel-injected engine. A four-speed gearbox arrived in April. **10.** Styling chief Bill Mitchell poses with the racing SR-2. **11.** Chevrolet built the SS (Super Sport) to race at Sebring, but it lasted only four hours.

11

# 1957 Pontiac

**1**

**2**

**4**

THE BREATH-TAKING

# BONNEVILLE

ANOTHER *Pontiac First!*

A SPECIAL LIMITED-EDITION
*Sports Convertible*
HAND-CRAFTED LUXURY
*plus* FUEL-INJECTION POWER

Feast your eyes on Pontiac's dream car to end all dream cars—the incomparable Bonneville! Here is the advanced creation that thrilled thousands who saw it at Daytona. Here, in a masterpiece of engineering, Pontiac combines brilliant styling and incredible luxury with the ultimate in modern V-8 performance . . . Fuel-Injection Power!

PONTIAC MOTOR DIVISION • GENERAL MOTORS CORPORATION

**3**

**1-2.** Pontiac went all-out with its new Bonneville convertible. Rochester fuel injection pumped the 370-cid V-8 to 310 horsepower, triggering Pontiac's performance image. No cheapie at $5782, it was the most potent Pontiac to date. Only 630 were built. **3.** Ads pushed Bonneville's "hand-crafted luxury" and "dream car" lineage. **4.** Star Chiefs again topped the regular line. **5.** Best-selling Star Chief was the Custom Catalina hardtop sedan. **6.** All wagons got a Safari name, but the dazzling two-door faced extinction.

**5**

**6**

1

2

3

4

6

5

1. Tri-Power engines were optional in any Pontiac, including this Chieftain sedan, rated 290 horsepower for street use. 2. If NASCAR-certified, the triple-carb V-8 delivered 317 horses. Cars so equipped got a heavy-duty suspension. As promoted in this ad, a strict-production Chieftain broke a track record in Grand National competition. Note the appearance of Pontiac general manager S. E. Knudsen, and styling director Harley J. Earl. 3. Two-door sedans, like this Chieftain, were prime candidates for the hottest V-8 engines. 4. Six- and nine-passenger Chieftain Safari station wagons went on sale. 5. Pontiac called its four-door Safari "a custom creation inside and out," with "man-sized comfort" and "barrel-chested Strato-Streak V-8." 6. Station wagons could be converted for ambulance and other commercial duty.

# 1957 Packard

## Studebaker-Packard Corporation

Packards now are built in South Bend, Indiana, alongside similar Studebakers

Designer Richard Teague turns ordinary Studebaker into patrician "Packardbaker," in hurry-up project

Supercharged V-8 engine goes into Packards—and Studebaker Golden Hawk . . . Packard's own engines are history

Clipper station wagon debuts—first Packard wagon since 1950

Packard lineup cut to just two offerings . . . sales plunge to only 4809

Studebaker Hawks adopt sweeping concave tailfins

Golden Hawk engine, force-fed by Paxton supercharger, makes 275 horsepower

Studebaker sedans/wagons get garish facelift

May brings budget-priced, no-frills Studebaker Scotsman—9300 built in just three months

Curtiss-Wright management agreement ends in October; Studebaker-Packard has had $85 million loss over three years

Studebaker-Packard loses $11 million this year, despite revived military production

Studebaker-Packard becomes North American distributor for Mercedes-Benz automobiles

1-2. Although the revered Packard name lingered on, it now identified a Studebaker clone. Only two models made the lineup: a Clipper four-door sedan (shown) selling for $3212, and a Country Sedan wagon. 3. Clippers, like their Studebaker first cousins, wore flamboyant fins. Taillights came from the '56 Clipper, grafted onto Studebaker fenders. Twin rear antennas were a styling touch from the departed Caribbean. Only 3940 sedans were produced. 4. Announcement of the Clipper was delayed until January. Planned as a stopgap, the move was supposed to "buy time" until a true Packard could be produced again—which never happened.

1

2

**1.** A mere 869 Clipper wagons were built, on a shorter wheelbase than the sedan.
**2.** A luggage rack cost $60 on a Country Sedan. Both body styles employed a Studebaker President chassis with a "proud Packard grille" and Caribbean-style trim.
**3.** Studebaker's new 275-horsepower, super-charged V-8 powered all Packards. Flight-O-Matic was standard and Twin Traction optional. **4.** Packards moved quickly from drawing board to production, but stylists had ideas for a new Caribbean. **5.** A "real" senior coupe might have looked like this.
**6.** A Clipper *not* based on the Studebaker would have had its own identity—perhaps even a convertible.

> 66 We are going to have a car. It may not be quite the car we hoped for, but it will be a lot better than what we feared. We'll go along. 99
>
> **Unidentified Packard dealer**, *on Studebaker-Packard's decision to bring out a Packard line for 1957; September 1956*

4

5

6

# 1957 Studebaker

1

3

2

4

5

**1-2.** Tailfins soared outward on the $3182 Golden Hawk. A fiberglass hood overlay hid a hole to clear the new super-charger. Just 4356 were built. **3.** With the new engine, a Hawk's front end was 100 pounds lighter. The blower gave five-psi boost, "for extra power the instant you need it." **4.** Studebaker planned to devote 25 percent of output to coupes. A Golden Hawk 400, added in spring, cost near-ly $500 extra but held hand-buffed leather. **5.** Golden Hawks had tooled instrument panels. **6.** Only two Hawk models were built, including the pillared Silver Hawk (either six-cylinder or V-8).

6

1

2

> 66 When you walked into that room full of cars, you walked into a new era of Studebaker-Packard progress—an era of profit for you and for us. 99
>
> *Studebaker-Packard president* **Harold E. Churchill**, *at S-P's annual stockholders' meeting; May 1957*

3

1. Studebaker sedans and wagons again came in three levels, topped by the President. 2. The $2666 Broadmoor station wagon was part of the President series. Its 289-cid V-8 yielded 210 or 225 horsepower. 3. Commander club sedans came in Custom or DeLuxe trim, with a 259-cid V-8. 4. This Parkview wagon served on police duty in South Bend, Indiana—Studebaker's home. 5. Studebaker had a full range, from low-budget Scotsman and Champion to hot Golden Hawk—one car that really was "unmistakably ahead of the rest." Scotsman models started at $1776, with miserly gearing and manual-shift only.

4

5

# 1958

Recession arrived with a vengeance to the shock and dismay of Americans who'd grown accustomed to prosperity. Inflation dipped below two percent, but unemployment approached and passed the seven-percent barrier. By June, 5,437,000 Americans were out of work—the highest figure since 1941.

Not that *everyone* was suffering. Those fortunate enough to have a full-time job might expect average earnings of $3851 per year. College teachers averaged $6015, and factory workers approached the $5000 mark. Dentists averaged more than $14,000, and the median family income reached $5087. Car prices rose 3.3 percent as the model year began, but the average amount paid for a new car actually dropped—to $2990, from $3230 a year earlier.

In the wake of Congressional hearings, the Automobile Information Disclosure Act was passed. From now on, window stickers would have to display every new vehicle's serial number and suggested retail price. Ever since, these documents have been known informally as "Monroney" stickers, after the U.S. senator largely responsible for the new law.

Nearly all cars were bigger and heavier (though use of aluminum grew 13 percent). Chrysler adopted compound-curve windshields that reached into the roofline. That worked fine, but their new fuel-injected engines did not. Practically all makes adopted quad-headlamp setups, and horsepower ratings rose an average of seven percent (20 bhp).

The biggest news of the year was the arrival of the Edsel, Ford's great hope for the mid-price field. The excitement, however, would be short-lived; in this recession era, yet another rather costly car—especially one whose styling drew as many guffaws as plaudits—just couldn't attract enough customers to survive.

Over at General Motors, this year's Buicks and Oldsmobiles were branded the most gaudy and garish vehicles of the year—if not the decade or the century. Chevrolets, on the other hand, exhibited a graceful restyling, led by the posh Impala—with an available hot new Turbo Thrust engine.

Packard departed after a last-ditch attempt to stay afloat by gussying up their Studebaker-based bodies even further. Henceforth, Studebaker would focus mainly on its compact Lark, ready for market ahead of shrunken rivals from the Big Three.

Imports took 8.1 percent of new-car sales—up more than tenfold since 1951—as the first Datsuns and Toyopets (Toyotas) arrived on the West Coast. George Romney turned AMC's full attention to compacts, including a revived reduced-size American. Still, many industry leaders echoed the thoughts of an anonymous GM executive: "If the public wants to lower its standard of living by driving a cheap crowded car, we'll make it."

In this worst economic setback of the postwar era, car sales dropped 31.4 percent for the model year. The influence of teenagers as car buyers was being noticed at last. A credit executive explained that at high schools, "far more students are car owners than most persons realize."

Alaska became the forty-ninth state. America's first satellite was launched from Cape Canaveral, and the Soviets countered with *Sputnik III*.

Economist John Kenneth Galbraith, in *The Affluent Society*, criticized the conformity and materialism of Americans. He also warned of decaying cities, driven through by gadget-laden autos. John Keats published *The Insolent Chariots*, a devastating but comic critique of the auto trade and car culture, featuring Tom Wretch doing battle with dealers.

Jack Kerouac's *On the Road*, first published a year earlier as a "beat generation" chronicle, began to attract more readers. Best-selling books ranged from *Anatomy of a Murder* and *Doctor Zhivago* to Art Linkletter's *Kids Say the Darndest Things!*

Elvis Presley was drafted into the U.S. Army. Folk music, after trailing far behind rock 'n' roll and jazz in popularity, began a resurgence, led by the Kingston Trio's recording of "Tom Dooley."

*The Donna Reed Show* appeared on TV, along with Chuck Connors in *The Rifleman*. So did *77 Sunset Strip* (co-starring Edd "Kookie" Byrnes, adored by female viewers more for his pompadour hairstyle than his acting skills). In a major scandal, quiz-show contestants pleaded guilty to having received answers ahead of time.

Moviegoers could see everything from Alfred Hitchcock's *Vertigo* to *Auntie Mame* and *Cat on a Hot Tin Roof*. Kim Stanley turned in a devastating performance as a movie queen in *The Goddess*, while Robert Mitchum drove hard through mountain roads as a whiskey runner in *Thunder Road*. Weekly movie admissions dipped below 40 million, the lowest figure since 1922—evidence of TV's impact.

Connie Francis sang "Who's Sorry Now," Peggy Lee belted out "Fever," and records could be played in stereo. Van Cliburn became the first American to win the top classical-music competition in Moscow.

Even though compacts were in the works at each Big Three auto company, the threat from such *sub*compacts as the Volkswagen Beetle and Renault Dauphine was deemed insignificant. The era of big barges had a few more years to go, and Detroit had another season of excess on the drawing board.

335

# 1958 Rambler

## American Motors Corporation

All models now grouped under Rambler nameplate (except Metropolitans)

Short-wheelbase Ramblers return, called American

Nearly 31,000 Americans are built in short model year

Regular Ramblers earn heavy facelift and sprout modest blade fins

All V-8s take Rebel nameplate; their 250-cid engine yields 215 horsepower

New Ambassador series debuts—it's actually an extended version of Rambler

Ambassador's V-8 engine is borrowed from departed full-size Nash/Hudson

Bigger model is called "Ambassador by Rambler," striving for separate identity

AMC touts '58s as the "world's finest travel cars"

New "deep-dip" rustproofing process sends unibodies into 15,000-gallon primer tank

Rambler reaches seventh spot in model-year production race—up from 12th in 1957

Metropolitan sales slip slightly to 13,128 units

AMC's new-car registrations more than double this year

Corporation earns $25.5 million profit

Ads claim that "no car is as strong—as safe—as quiet"

1

2

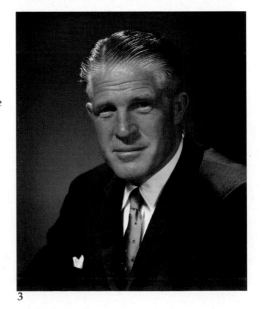

3

1. At mid-season, AMC revived its 100-inch-wheelbase model, now called American. Prices started at $1775 for a business sedan, but this Super went for $1874. A 90-horsepower six-cylinder engine promised up to 30 mpg. 2. Americans came only in two-door form, topped by this Super. Few options were offered beyond overdrive, Flash-O-Matic, radio, and heater. 3. AMC president George Romney earned credit for the daring revival of the small Rambler, unseen for three years. Except for a new grille and enlarged rear wheel openings, it looked similar to the '55 model. Romney had neither time nor money to come up with an all-new design, but Americans arrived at an opportune moment: during a recession, as imports were capturing serious sales.

336

❝Auto buyers are getting choosy, backing away from dreamboats to look for something more practical.❞

*Consumers Union head of automobile testing* **Laurence E. Crooks**, *on the changing tastes of new-car buyers; April 1958*

**1.** American interiors were simple, but not stark. **2.** The American got its own brochure, where it claimed to "put real fun back into motoring." **3.** AMC stretched the Rambler nine inches ahead of the cowl to create a new Ambassador. **4.** Called a "living room" on wheels, an Ambassador Custom could get 20 trim combinations. **5.** AMC's four-door models included the Rambler Six, Rebel V-8, and new Ambassador V-8. **6.** Only 1340 Ambassador Custom Country Club hardtop sedans were sold. **7.** Metropolitans continued with few changes, but prices rose by $59 to $1626 for the coupe, $1650 for the convertible.

# 1958 Rambler

1

1-2. All Rebels, including this four-door hardtop, were V-8 powered. AMC's 250-cid engine made 215 horsepower. Ramblers wore a low grille and quad headlights in the normal position. The side trim on upscale models was reminiscent of final Hudsons. 3. This cutaway demonstrates how six people fit inside a Rambler. Single Unit Construction, ads stated, was "pioneered by American Motors—and now copied by others in the very highest price car lines." AMC claimed that it "offers the greatest strength, durability and safety ever known," because huge box girders completely surrounded the occupants. During manufacturing, 9000 electric welds replaced the old-fashioned body bolts to eliminate squeaks and rattles.

2

3

1

1. Station wagons were always crucial to the Rambler lineup. This pointy-finned Rebel four-door wagon came in Super or Custom trim.
2. AMC promoted the fact that its Economy six-cylinder engine held official NASCAR border-to-border and coast-to-coast economy records—33.93 and 32.09 mpg, respectively. The six made 127 horsepower, but optional dual-throat carburetion hiked output to 138 horses. Ads insisted a Rebel would mix "Rambler handling and parking ease with smooth, economical V-8 performance," branded "velvety" at cruising speeds. 3-4. Ads promised that Ramblers delivered an appetizing blend of big-car comfort and roominess, plus imported-car economy. The compacts could also "turn on a dime," unlike typical American sedans and wagons, and appealed to the "little woman."

2

3

4

> **"**I'd just as soon see the public educated as to the actual cost price of a new car so that we could get the confusion out of the selling price. The way it is now, most buyers have a fantastic idea of how much money a dealer can make from selling a car. **"**
>
> **Unidentified**
> **Missouri new-car dealer;**
> *September 1958*

# Chrysler Corporation

Chrysler products begin to abandon Hemi V-8s, turning to simpler—and cheaper—wedge-head configuration

Double compound, triple-curve Control-Tower wind-shields extend into roofline

Chrysler 300-D engine delivers 380 or 390 horsepower; hardtop and convertible offered

Bendix fuel injection offered—briefly—on 300-D engine, but complex unit proves troublesome

Privately-owned 300-D sets new Class E speed record at Bonneville, running 156.387 mph

Automatic speed control offered on Chrysler and Imperial

Chrysler Division dips to 11th place in the industry as output drops by nearly half

DeSoto output shrinks below 50,000—lowest since 1938

Nearly all fuel-injected engines are later fitted with carburetors

Imperial output drops to 16,113 cars—down by more than half

Any Plymouth may have the new Golden Commando 350-cid engine

Plymouth ends year in third place again, ahead of Oldsmobile and Buick

Experimental Plymouth Cabana hardtop features sliding sunroof

1. Little-changed overall, Chrysler New Yorkers wore new bodyside trim. This sedan cost $4295. The 392-cid V-8 produced 345 horsepower. Chryslers exemplified "the bold new look of success," according to the brochure. 2. Saratogas carried a 310-horsepower, 354-cid engine. The sedan cost $3818. 3. A 290-bhp version of the 354-cid V-8 went into Windsors, including this $3214 hardtop, which dropped to the 122-inch Dodge wheelbase. 4. The most popular Chrysler was the $3129 Windsor four-door sedan, with 12,861 produced. 5. As part of its push in the spring selling season, Chrysler issued Windsors with Dartline styling, "bright and cheerful as spring itself." Three gold crowns embellished a brushed aluminum insert.

GLEEM
the toothpaste for people who
can't brush after every meal!

> "The really modern automobile should convey an eager, poised-for-action look."
>
> *Chrysler Corp. styling vice-president* **Virgil Exner**, *on the corporation's "Forward Look" design philosophy; December 1958*

1-2. Tall fins dominated the profile of the Chrysler New Yorker hardtop, which cost $4347. 3. Oddly shrunken taillights no longer filled the big tailfin cavities. 4. All entrants in this Gleem toothpaste contest had to do to win a new Chrysler was to estimate the total retail price of all items pictured. 5. The 392-cid V-8 in a Chrysler 300-D put out 380 or 390 bhp. A hardtop sold for $5173, the convertible for $5603. Only 809 were built. 6. Drivers faced large round gauges with a clock between. Round control knobs ran along the bottom, and TorqueFlite buttons were at the left. 7. Chrysler promoted the glamorous aspects of its "mighty" models.

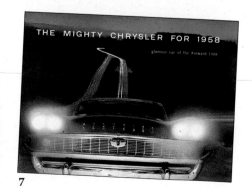

THE MIGHTY CHRYSLER FOR 1958

# 1958 DeSoto

1. DeSoto's lineup included the Fireflite (*foreground*), Firedome (*upper left*), and budget-priced Firesweep (*upper right*).
2. Stacked taillights made DeSotos easy to spot. Only 3243 Fireflite Sportsman four-door hardtops were built, starting at $3731. The 361-cid V-8 developed 305 horsepower. Note the curiously pinched exhaust outlets.
3. A Fireflite ragtop went for $3972, but only 474 folks got one.  4. Just $3219 bought a Firesweep convertible, new this season.
5. Can these Goodyears both be 14-inch tires? The new 11.00x14 luxury tire and 7.50x14 size represented the extremes on 1958 cars. The 11.00x14 tire ran at only 14–17 pounds of air pressure.

1. A DeSoto Adventurer two-door hardtop started at $4071, but the convertible commanded $298 more. This hardtop has rare spinner hubcaps and gold-fleck carpeting. All DeSotos got a more complex grille.

2. Under an Adventurer hood, DeSoto's 361-cid V-8 yielded 345 or 355 horsepower—the latter via complex (and finicky) Bendix fuel injection, which cost $637 extra. Most of the few fuel-injected models sold were later converted to dual carburetors, signaling the end of that experiment.

3. Only 350 Adventurer hardtops and a mere 82 ragtops were produced.

4. DeSotos had long been popular for use as commercial vehicles, so specialty manufacturers converted an ordinary sedan into an eight-door stretch limo. Note the extra-long roof luggage rack.

2    1

3

4

# 1958 Dodge

1. Dodge's mild facelift included a fresh grille and simplified side trim. At midyear came a new top-of-the-line model, the specially trimmed $3245 Regal Lancer two-door hardtop. 2. The Regal Lancer's plush, color-keyed interior sported a selection of notable touches, including ribbed door trim panels with molded-in armrests, bronze instrument cluster, and glovebox trim bevels. 3-4. Regal Lancers came only in metallic bronze with contrasting black roof, fins, and color sweep; or in a blend of bronze and white. Just 1163 were produced. The 350-cid engine made 285 horsepower. 5. A Custom Royal Lancer convertible cost $3298.

❝Why put up with the old buggy?  $75 down at Sanford's buys a new 1958 Dodge or Plymouth. ❞

**Ad copy, Pittsburgh new-car dealer**; *January 1958*

**1**

**2**

**3**

**4**

**5**

1. Dodge's open Custom Royal Lancer sold slowly, as only 1139 rolled off the line. 2. Instrument panels held a horizontal-sweep speedometer and dash-mounted mirror. 3. Dual exhausts were fitted to the $3142 four-door Custom Royal Lancer. Red Ram and Super Red Ram V-8s grew to 252 and 265 horsepower. New Ram-Fire V-8s came in 350-cid size, or 361 cid in the D-500 and Super D-500 options. 4. Not too many shoppers got a "spring edition" of the Coronet Lancer, sporting a textured-insert chrome spear. This one has a six-cylinder engine with stickshift. 5. Dodge's most popular wagon was the Sierra. 6. New "knockout" colors, special trim, and "bewitching" interiors marked "Spring Swept-Wing" models. 7. Celebrities such as actress/singer Debbie Reynolds liked the Italian-bodied, Dodge-powered Dual-Ghia. 8. Strong engines made Coronets the choice of the Missouri State Highway Patrol.

**6**

**7**

**8**

# 1958 Imperial

1

1. Ten mildly facelifted Imperial models were issued, from base sedan and hardtops to the seldom-seen Crown Imperial limo. This Southampton Crown hardtop coupe cost $5388. **2.** Imperials, including this Crown convertible, were two inches longer and held a 345-horsepower, 392-cid V-8. **3.** Touch-up work included a fresh six-section grille below quad headlights. **4.** The most popular Imperial was the Crown four-door hardtop, with 4146 built. Note the unique landau roof section. Options included electric door locks, Auto-Pilot automatic driver assist (an early cruise control), and Super Soft Cushion tires. **5.** With the exception of the limo, LeBaron served as the top-rung Imperial. It was offered as a pillared or hardtop sedan for $5969. **6.** Like all luxury makes, Imperials had to be leakproof.

2

3

4

6

5

1

6

7

2

3

4

5

1. A simplified front end led Plymouth's detail changes. This Belvedere Sport Sedan has a PowerPak V-8. 2. A Belvedere Sport Coupe cost $2457. 3. Belvedere four-door sedans sold best. 4. Only 4229 Belvedere Club Sedans went to customers. 5. Belvedere convertibles came standard with V-8 power. 6. Another Fury stormed in, aiming at "the man who really loves cars." 7. Fury promised a blend of "family car comfort" and "capabilities of a true competition car."

# 1958 Plymouth

1

2

6

7

3

4

"It's a rich man's kind of car...but my kind of price!"

"I might be a rich man myself some day . . . but why wait! I feel like one right now in my new Plymouth! It has the luxury and features of cars costing thousands more. It *looks* like a rich man's car, it *rides* like a rich man's car. And it's right in the low-price 3! No wonder they're saying: there's no catching Plymouth!"

• SILVER DART STYLING • TORSION-AIRE RIDE • GOLDEN COMMANDO V-8* • DIRECTIONAL STABILIZER FINS • PUSH-BUTTON TORQUEFLITE*

*optional at low extra cost

Star of the Forward Look **Plymouth** ...ahead for keeps!

5

1-2. Sportone trim with anodized aluminum inserts decorates this Plymouth Belvedere Sport Coupe. **3.** Dashboards showed little change, with four round gauges flanking the large speedometer. Note the two-tone upholstery and top-of-dash mirror. **4.** The 318-cid V-8 developed 225 horsepower in standard form, or 250 with a four-barrel carburetor. **5.** Low price sold many a Plymouth, but the new Golden Commando engine attracted a different breed of customer. Sales dropped 42 percent, but Plymouth remained in third place—not quite "ahead for keeps," as ads suggested. **6.** The top-selling Plymouth was the Savoy four-door sedan, with 67,933 built. This one has the 132-horsepower six-cylinder engine and stickshift, as well as standard bodyside chrome. **7.** Nearly as dashing as a Belvedere, especially with Sportone trim, the Savoy Sport Coupe cost $128 less.

**Trunk, '58 Plymouth, cleaned *and* waxed**

VISTA TIME: 6 minutes
DURATION: up to 6 months

Simoniz makes it as only Simoniz can—VISTA, for tough *real* paste wax beauty and protection. VISTA is *real* paste wax with cleaner in it—*turbo-whipped* so it spreads smoothly, dries and wipes off quickly. One easy application cleans, shines and protects your car for months...*try it*. SIMONIZ MAKES IT

"We're not the richest people in town...but we're the proudest!"

Star of the Forward Look **Plymouth** ...ahead for keeps!

1. Posh or practical, wagons epitomized the suburban lifestyle. Plymouth's Custom Suburban looked ordinary with basic trim and blackwalls but had ample oomph with V-8 power. This one has TorqueFlite and air conditioning. 2. Simonizing a Plymouth trunk might be accomplished in six minutes, but waxing the whole car took a lot more time and "elbow grease." 3. Rear-facing third seats attracted plenty of families with children. Seven Suburban wagon models went on sale, accounting for more than 28 percent of production. 4. Americans were proud of their Plymouths—or any new car they drove home. Automobiles served as an easy indicator of a family's status. 5. Not many people paid $500 extra for fuel injection, and those who did were sorry when the mechanical unit proved unruly. 6. Kids started driving Plymouths early—if they had pedal-power. 7. Low-priced Plazas made practical police cars.

POLICE

351

# 1958 Edsel

# Ford Motor Company

Long-rumored mid-price Edsel debuts amid a hail of publicity

Ford now has a five-model lineup, comparable to GM's

Edsel is positioned between Ford and Mercury

22,000 Edsels ready at launch—20 per dealer— "priced where you want it"

Edsels feature pushbutton automatic transmission in steering wheel

Edsel sales fail to take off— launch takes place just as national recession begins and mid-price market has sagged

Ford issues unibodied four-passenger Thunderbird

New "Squarebird" pioneers personal-luxury concept, and outsells original two-seater

Facelifted Ford offers new three-speed Cruise-O-Matic transmission, plus FE-series big-block V-8s

Lincoln adopts unibody construction, but weight goes up instead of down

Mark III Continental is Lincoln-based

Lincoln's 430-cid V-8 is biggest U.S. engine; also available in Mercury

About 100 Fords have optional air suspension— units prove to be problematic

Mercury offers three-speed Multi-Drive transmission

The EDSEL LOOK is here to stay
—and 1959 cars will prove it!

All Detroit knows it—next year's big style change is the fresh, distinctive styling that Edsel has right now! So step into the car that has future written all over it. And discover how the future is also *built into* it! Only Edsel Teletouch Drive puts the shift buttons where they belong, on the steering-wheel hub. Only Edsel gives you high-economy 303 and 345 hp V-8 engines. Only Edsel gives you comfort-shaped contour seats, Dial-temp heating, self-adjusting brakes, along with many other exclusive advances. So get the car with the advanced design that makes it worth more now —worth more when you finally trade it in. And get the magnificent Edsel at a surprisingly low price. There's less than fifty dollars difference between Edsel and V-8's in the Low-Priced Three.* See your Edsel Dealer. EDSEL DIVISION • FORD MOTOR COMPANY

Less than fifty dollars difference between Edsel and V-8's in the Low-Priced Three

*Based on comparison of manufacturers' suggested retail delivered prices.

1

**1.** During the design process, there was reason to believe that Edsel styling was "here to stay." Mid-price sales had been booming, but by the time Edsels debuted, that market had shrunk substantially. Ford hoped to sell 100,000 in the first year, but built just over 63,000. **2.** Rumored for two years, the Edsel turned out less radical than expected—but critics found amusing (and crude) words to describe the "horse-collar" grille. **3.** Vice President Richard Nixon greets the crowd from an Edsel in Lima, Peru.

2

3

1. Company president Henry Ford II had reason to smile when he first took the wheel of an Edsel, but hope turned to disaster as the car failed to attract buyers. Benson and William Clay Ford ride along on this publicity trip. 2. Edsel's 18-model lineup included three top-rung Citations, twin Corsairs, four Pacers, and four budget-priced Rangers—plus station wagons. 3. More than most '58 cars, the Edsel's "distinctive" appearance was indeed recognizable from a distance, as this ad claimed. 4. After pondering 6000 possible names for the new make, Ford chose to honor Edsel Ford, who'd passed on in 1943. Edsel was the only son of the company's founder, and the father of Henry Ford II. 5. Basic engineering followed corporate trends, but the cars could be packed with gadgets. Once on sale, Edsels were actually faulted for being over-powered, especially with the bigger engine. 6. Ford design chief George Walker (*left*) and Benson Ford posed in the design studio with Edsel manager Richard Krafve (standing). Note the work being done on a full-size clay model, which looks close to final form.

# 1958 Edsel

1

4

2

5

3

1-2. An Edsel Citation convertible sold for $3801, but only 930 were built. Like most upper models, this one is loaded, including the 410-cid V-8 and Teletouch automatic. Note the slim, wide horizontal taillights. 3. J. C. Whitney, the Chicago parts supplier, soon added Edsel extras to its catalog. 4. A Corsair hardtop is pictured at the Proving Grounds prior to launch date. 5. The cheapest Edsel, at $2519, was the Ranger two-door sedan. 6. In publicity photos, at least, engineers wore serious-looking white coats. Here, a pack of Pacers takes to the test track.

> **"** The Edsel is our 'idea car.' The basic target is to continue to give the public outstanding performance and operating economy. **"**
>
> *Mercury-Edsel-Lincoln general manager* **James J. Nance**; *March 1958*

6

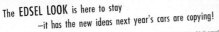

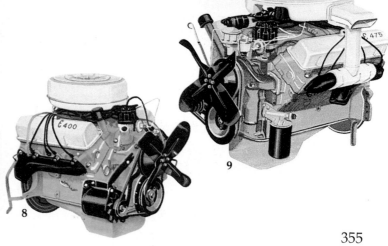

**1.** An Edsel Pacer convertible went for $773 less than the Citation version, and sold twice as well. **2.** Teletouch Drive put transmission pushbuttons in the steering wheel. **3.** Dashboards followed aircraft practice, with instruments, controls, and warning lights in three horizontal rows. Edsels used a "cyclops eye" rotating-drum speedometer. **4.** It's true that "Edsel dared to break out of the lookalike rut," but the new look wouldn't last nearly as long as Ford expected—and "next year's cars" wouldn't be copying its stylistic touches. **5.** Part of the Pacer series, the Bermuda wagon could be fitted for six or nine passengers. **6.** Kids could slip easily into the rear of a Bermuda wagon. **7.** The E-196X was supposed to illustrate a possible evolution of the 1958 Edsel's front-end theme. Here, Edsel executive stylist I. B. Kaufman (*left*) explains the potential of the vertical-grille design to styling director George Walker. **8.** Edsel's E-400 engine, used in the Pacer and Ranger series (and all wagons), delivered 303 horsepower. **9.** Citations and Corsairs used the 345-horsepower, 410-cid E-475 engine.

1

2

3

4

**66** The styling sections make it very difficult for the engineers to produce a trouble-free car. Styling has gone too extreme. All this lowness and extra sculpturing are bringing a lot of things we don't want. **99**

**Unidentified Ford dealer**, *on the engineering problems vexing new-car dealers and buyers; May 1958*

1-2. Ford's fully facelifted Fairlane 500 Club Victoria cost $2435. Oval taillights sat in a newly sculpted deck. Grooves went into roof panels, and hoods held a fake scoop. 3. A Fairlane 500 Sunliner convertible cost $2650. Several features of this year's restyle were done not with beauty in mind, but to increase body-panel strength. 4. Fender skirts and a Continental kit added extra flash to the Ford Fairlane's shape. 5. Naturally, the J. C. Whitney catalog held temptations for Ford owners. Thousands of car fans pored through the small-print pages of each catalog as it arrived in the mail.

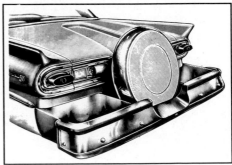

5

1. Production of Ford's Fairlane 500 Skyliner retractable hardtop coupe dropped to 14,713 cars, priced at $3163. 2. More than 135,000 Custom 300 Fordor sedans went on sale. The popular model started at $2159. 3. Custom 300, Ford's second-cheapest series, included only Tudor and Fordor sedans. 4. Styled earlier in the decade, the experimental FX Atmos looked more at home in a sci-fi movie than on any street—especially with those protruding spears. 5. This scene in Oak Park, Illinois, is typical of suburban business streets in the late '50s. Note '58 Fairlane at right.

> "Ford surveys find only a limited place for the little car and no evidence that the American public is interested in lowering its standard of living by buying an economy car on a large scale."
>
> *Mercury-Edsel-Lincoln general manager* **James J. Nance**, *justifying Detroit's reluctance to aggressively enter the small-car market; April 1958*

# 1958 Lincoln

1

2

3

4

5

6

7

1. Bearing no resemblance to the graceful Mark II, the heavily sculpted Continental Mark III came in four body styles. This Landau hardtop sedan cost $6072.
2. Lincolns and Mercurys took their turns for testing at the Proving Grounds. 3. A pillared Continental Mark III sedan cost the same as the hardtop, but only 1283 were built. 4. Just over 3000 customers paid $6283 to grab an open Continental. 5. A Lincoln Premiere Landau hardtop cost $5505. To cope with heavier structures, Lincoln enlarged its V-8 to 430 cid—the biggest in America—making 375 bhp. 6. A Lincoln Premiere looked little different than costlier Continentals. 7. Premiere four-door sedans failed to sell well.

❝Domestic cars are awful, particularly the styling. ❞

**Unidentified Los Angeles import-car dealer**, *on why he chose to sell imports instead of a domestic make; September 1958*

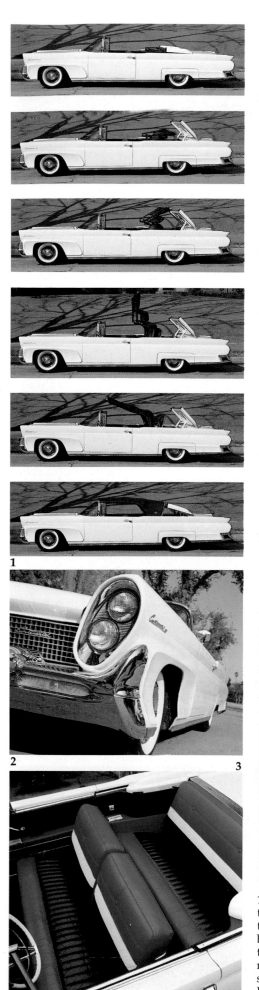

1. The new Continental's top-stowage setup borrowed ideas from Ford's retractable hard-top. A metal panel raised out of the way, allowing the top to raise or lower. Lack of a protruding boot accentuated the long lines. Soon dubbed "land yachts," these were the biggest Continentals ever. 2. Slanted housings held quad headlights. Structurally identical to Lincolns, Continentals had their own grille and reverse-slant rear window. 3. Continentals carried fine fabrics or Bridge of Weir leather from Scotland. 4. Lincoln's Capri series cost about $500 less than the Premiere. 5. Not quite a superstar just yet, Elvis Presley took the wheel of a Mark III. 6. Vice President Richard M. Nixon served as Grand Marshal of this Aquatennial parade, riding in a Continental convertible with wife Pat.

# 1958 Buick

## General Motors Corporation

GM celebrates 50th anniversary

Buick revives Limited series—a badge unused since the 1940s

Flight Pitch triple-turbine Dynaflow debuts in Buicks

Buick sinks to fifth place in production, behind Oldsmobile, as output drops 40 percent

Buick dealers now sell German-built Opel; Pontiac dealers get British Vauxhall

Chevrolets and Pontiacs adopt all-coil suspensions

Chevrolet adds luxury Impala

Full-size Chevrolets may have Turbo Thrust 348-cid V-8

Chevrolet captures 30 percent of market—a record figure

Demand for restyled Corvette sports cars rises smartly—to 9168 cars

Each make offers air suspension; unit proves troublesome, and many are converted to springs

Garishly reworked Oldsmobiles look bigger and heavier

Triple-carb J-2 option boosts Oldsmobile's V-8 to 312 bhp

All Pontiacs hold Bonneville-sized 370-cid V-8

Buicks and Oldsmobiles get new one-piece rear windows

1

2

3

It's easy to see

why mothers like this Buick

First big car that's light on its feet

the AIR BORN B-58 BUICK

5

4

1. Buick's Limited Riviera hardtop sedan listed at $5112 ($33 higher than a Series 62 Cadillac). Though two inches shorter in wheelbase than a Caddy, the Buick was longer overall. 2. Limiteds wore more brightwork than other Buicks, but all flaunted a studded Dynastar grille. 3. Twin-Tower taillights helped give the Limited convertible a distinctive stance. 4. This special "Wells Fargo" Limited was built for Dale Robertson, star of the Buick-sponsored *Tales of Wells Fargo* TV show. 5. Ads lauded visibility through the huge wraparound back window.

It's the "HIS" and "HER" car

—first big car that's light on its feet

Big·Bold·Buoyant
the AIR BORN B-58 BUICK

1. Overwrought and overchromed, Buick's open Century epitomized the age of excess.
2. Hardtop station wagons came in the Century (shown) and Special series.
3. Buick promised glamour and easy handling for her, robust behavior for him.
4. A Special Riviera hardtop sedan cost $2820, but this body style was issued in all five series. 5. Buick and Olds bodyshells leave the welding jig at Ionia Manufacturing Co., the supplier of station wagon bodies. 6. General manager Edward T. Ragsdale displays the *Sports Car Illustrated* Award for safety. Buick was first to employ aluminum brake drums.

# 1958 Cadillac

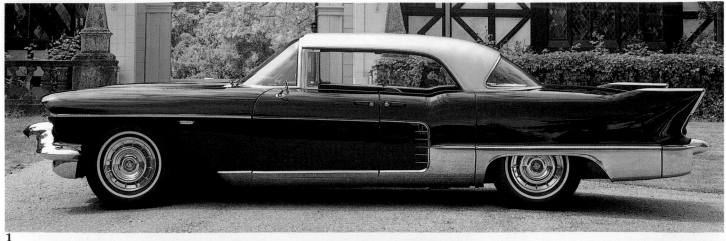

1

2

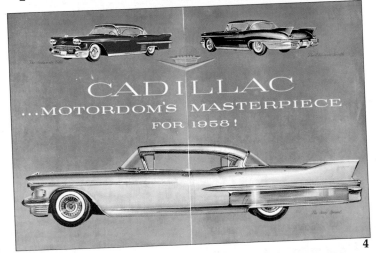

3

1. Again priced at $13,074, the Eldorado Brougham showed little change apart from new wheel covers. 2. Only 304 Broughams were built. This car spent its early life in Holland. 3. Brougham door panels switched from metal finish to leather.

4

5

6

4. Not everyone dubbed the '58 Cadillac a "masterpiece." Sheetmetal got only minor reshaping with spiked fins, but these were the most flamboyant Cadillacs yet, gushing with chrome. Shown: a Sedan de Ville, Eldorado Seville, and Sixty Special. 5. Rather than issue special editions to mark its Golden Anniversary, GM merely promoted a typical example from each of the five makes. 6. Portraying a raucous-living rancher with a stupefying lack of scruples, Paul Newman drove his Cadillac convertible hard in the 1962 movie *Hud*. In one scene, the car nearly leaps into the air as it crosses a railroad track at breakneck speed.

**1.** Few convertibles had air conditioning in 1958, not to mention walrus-hide upholstery. This Eldorado Biarritz has both. **2.** A Biarritz brought an even $7500 this season—same price as the Seville hardtop coupe. Eldorado engines adopted triple two-barrel carburetors, boosting output to 335 horsepower. Other models made do with a single four-barrel carb and 310 bhp. **3.** Sedan de Villes ranked as the top Cadillac sellers. Series 62 added a hardtop sedan with an extended rear deck, which sold almost as well. **4.** Tradition still played a major role in attracting customers to Cadillac. Ads implied that arrival at a classy resort or restaurant was best accomplished in a fancy automobile. **5.** Even Cadillacs had to have their oil checked periodically. Visitors to this gas station near Pensacola, Florida, got a free beverage while they waited.

1

2

3

4

IT OUTSTEPS ITS OWN GREAT TRADITIONS!

The statement above represents the finest compliment that could be paid a Cadillac car. Yet, we feel it is a compliment that is richly deserved. For in every way, this newest "car of cars" represents a step beyond its own high standards of excellence. Most certainly, it deserves your personal appraisal. We suggest that you let your dealer introduce you to Cadillac's exclusive Fleetwood coachcrafting—and bring you up to date on all the new models, including the distinguished new Eldorado Brougham.

CADILLAC MOTOR CAR DIVISION • GENERAL MOTORS CORPORATION
Every Window of Every Cadillac is Safety Plate Glass

*Cadillac*

5

# 1958 Oldsmobile

1

2

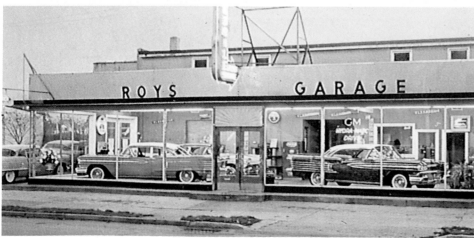

4

3

1. Thin-pillar styling made it hard to tell an Olds Ninety-Eight sedan from the stronger-selling Holiday hardtop. Sharply slanted windshield pillars were responsible for many sore shins. 2. An Olds Ninety-Eight ragtop cost $4300. Most sheetmetal was new, but the cars lost their styling continuity. 3. Budget-conscious couples had to cut corners where they could. Hot-tip AC plugs promised to save up to one gallon of gas in every ten. 4. Each series included a convertible. The Super 88 went for $3529. 5. Boasting a typical look for the times, this showroom was in Williamstown, New Jersey.

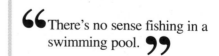

5

❝There's no sense fishing in a swimming pool.❞

*Unidentified **Seattle new-car dealer**, on his unwillingness to undertake elaborate promotions in a depressed economic climate; February 1958*

# Oldsmobile 1958

1. A fleet of Oldsmobile Ninety-Eight convertibles marked the opening of the Mackinac Bridge, linking Michigan's upper and lower peninsulas. 2. A newly optional Trans-Portable Radio slipped out of its slot in the Fashion-Flare dash to run on its own batteries. Note the pull handle and lock. 3. Just $3262 could buy a Super 88 Holiday hardtop, but this coupe is loaded with extras—skirts, outside spare, and J-2 Tri-Power engine. 4. Super 88 Holiday hardtops sold well, with 18,653 built. 5. The 88 series included both a regular four-door sedan—the top Oldsmobile seller—and a pillarless Holiday hardtop. 6. Fiesta wagons came in pillared or hardtop form. 7. The six-millionth Oldsmobile, a Holiday Ninety-Eight four-door hardtop, was built on November 8, 1957.

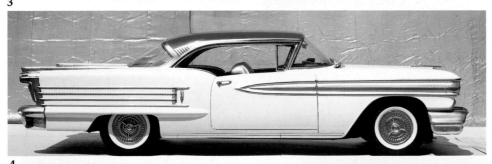

> 66 With one out of every seven American workers dependent directly or indirectly upon the automobile industry for his livelihood, the effect of this decrease in automobile sales in aggravating and deepening the current recession should be obvious. 99
>
> *Tennessee senator*
> **Estes Kefauver**; *March 1958*

# 1958 Pontiac

1

2

3

4

5

6

1. Pontiac's flagship Bonneville, billed as "America's hot road car," rode the Chieftain's shorter 122-inch wheelbase. 2. An external spare-tire mount and super-hot 330-bhp Tri-Power engine added extra bucks to the $3586 tariff of a Bonneville convertible—Pontiac's costliest model. Just 3096 were built. 3. Dazzling upholstery in a Bonneville ragtop comprised "hand-buffed glove-soft cowhides" to match the body color. This car has the Tri-Power triple carburetion option. 4. Pontiac issued 9144 Bonneville Sport Coupes, starting at $3481. This one has Rochester fuel-injection, a $500 option. Bonneville hardtops had a fake vent above the rear window, like Chevrolet's Impala. 5. Pontiac's Chieftain and Star Chief series included Safari wagons, promising "road-wedded stability." 6. Testing under NASCAR auspices bore out Pontiac's claim to be America's top road car. Sporting a fresh "New Direction" look, Pontiacs measured up to 8.7 inches longer and 4.5 inches lower.

1

2

3

**1-3.** In Pontiac's entry-level Chieftain series, a Catalina hardtop cost $2707. Though less lavish than upper models, Chieftains were generously chromed. The gas cap hid behind the left backup light. **4.** Leather was a no-cost option on the $3122 Star Chief Custom Catalina hardtop, billed as "Luxury Unlimited." **5.** Only 2905 Star Chief Custom Safaris—Pontiac's top wagon—went on sale at $3350. This one has Tri-Power. **6.** This special Bonneville was upholstered with 11 African leopard pelts. Stylist Sandra Longyear wears a then-fashionable leopard coat for the publicity photo. **7.** A Tri-Power Bonneville convertible, driven by Sam Hanks, paced the Indy 500 race on May 30.

4

5

6

7

> **"** If all cars were 1958 models, we would be in trouble. **"**
>
> *Norfolk, Virginia, city traffic engineer* **Fenton G. Jordan,** *on a street-parking crisis caused by 1958 automobiles too long to fit comfortably into prepainted parking spaces; January 1958*

# Studebaker-Packard Corporation

Last Packards go on sale exhibiting hasty restyle

Packard Hawk is strange luxury version of Studebaker Golden Hawk, sporting outside armrests and simulated spare tire

Studebaker-Packard announces halt to Packard production in mid-season

Studebaker President and Commander series add hardtop-coupe body style

Each Studebaker series trims its lineup

Studebaker sedans and wagons (except Scotsman) get grafted-on tailfins and quad headlights

Like most '58 makes, Studebakers are longer and lower, with Flight Stream roofline

Fender vent doors are gone, replaced by cowl ventilation

Little-changed no-frills Scotsman series sells well

Studebaker Golden Hawk output skids to 878 cars, far below the total for Silver Hawk

Only 44,759 Studebakers are produced in the U.S., for 14th-place ranking

Packard ranks dead last, far behind Continental, with only 2622 cars built

Studebaker-Packard loses $13 million for the year

1. Chief stylist Duncan McRae designed the '58 Packards swiftly and cheaply—in most eyes, an ignominious end to the once-grand marque. McRae mainly grafted extra pieces—fins and pod-mounted quad headlights—onto the existing body to differentiate it from the so-similar Studebaker.
2. Studebaker's Golden Hawk and the new Packard Hawk were the only supercharged production cars in America. The variable-speed centrifugal blower delivered up to 5-psi boost to the 275-horsepower V-8.
3. Only 588 Packard Hawks were produced, with a $3995 sticker price—$700 higher than the Golden Hawk and $300 above a Corvette. A Hawk could accelerate to 60 mph in about eight seconds.

> ❝Our job is far from easy and the current recession has made it all the harder.❞
>
> *Studebaker-Packard president* **Harold E. Churchill**, *addressing S-P stockholders about the corporation's sales woes; April 1958*

1

2

4

3

5

> **66**In the opinion of your management, without this plan the chance of restoring any real value to your stock is practically nonexistent. **99**
>
> *Studebaker-Packard president* **Harold E. Churchill**, *on a refinancing and diversification program intended to bolster S-P's fortunes; September 1958*

**1-2.** A 210-horsepower rendition of Studebaker's 289-cid V-8 went into other Packard models, including the new Starlight hardtop. An automatic transmission was standard. Just 675 hardtops rolled off the line, priced at $3262. Note the two-step outward-leaning tailfins—a fin atop a fin. **3.** Packard Hawks stuck with single headlights instead of the trendy four-light setup installed on other models. A low, full-width grille opening gave the Hawk's long, bolt-on fiberglass nose a puzzled grin. **4.** Hawk dashboards held small round gauges on a tooled panel. Based upon the posh '57 Studebaker Golden Hawk 400, Packard Hawks had leather interiors and extra trim—including unique exterior vinyl padding on door tops. **5.** Hawk decklids displayed a simulated spare tire, and tailfins held mylar inserts. **6.** The rarest '58 Packard of all is the $3384 station wagon, with a mere 159 produced. Note the four headlights, stuck into twin pods tacked onto the fenders.

6

# 1958 Studebaker

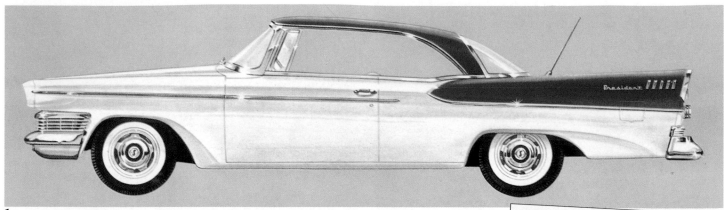

1

2

4

1. Studebaker added a hardtop coupe to its President and Commander series. Billed as "scintillating," this Starlight President cost $2695. 2-3. Not much change was evident in the supercharged Golden Hawk, except for 14-inch tires and optional air conditioning. 4. Studebaker promoted the "Hawk-inspired" styling of its full-size models. 5. Presidents got 14-inch wheels and a 225-bhp engine. 6. Part of the Commander series, the Provincial wagon cost $2664 and used a smaller 259-cid, 180-bhp V-8. 7. A Commander hardtop cost $202 less than its President cousin. 8. Commanders came in three body styles, including the $2378 sedan.

3

5

6

7

8

378

1-3. Studebaker's Champion dropped to a sedan-only lineup. This four-door sold for $2253. The 185.6-cid L-head six-cylinder engine again put out 101 horsepower. Pod-mounted quad headlights were optional on Champions, standard on upper models, but not available at all on the low-budget Scotsman. Flight-O-Matic was optional, but plenty of Champions had stickshift or over-drive. 4. Champion dashboards had a basic look with small gauges. Flight-Style instrument panels featured a Magna-Dial speedometer and Safety-Cone steering wheel. Studebaker promoted the safety of its cars, interior space, variable-rate front springs, and variable-ratio steering. 5. A no-trim Scotsman two-door sedan went for just $1795, while the four-door version cost $1874. Scotsman models accounted for 38 percent of total production. 6. The Scotsman station wagon cost $2055. Ads promised three-way economy: when buying, driving, and reselling.

1959

f any year serves as the consummate example of Fifties immoderation, it has to be 1959. Cadillac tailfins reached as tall as they ever would, and virtually every other make's stretched only a little shorter. Chevrolet sent its fins soaring outward instead of skyward, but they served the same dubious purpose. Buick also took the sideways route with its new "delta-wing" styling, and each upper GM make adopted a massive rear "picture window." GM also increased the use of shared bodyshells.

Ignoring the troubles GM had experienced with air suspensions, Chrysler launched its own version this year. Studebaker dropped the hot Golden Hawk but issued a more modest Silver Hawk coupe.

After arriving on the market with such promise and potential a year earlier, Edsel was already on the ropes. A handful of 1960 models were issued, built late this year; after which the name survived only as a virtual synonym for mammoth failure. Engines continued to grow in size and strength as the horsepower race wore on. Chrysler abandoned the legendary Hemi V-8 engine but had a selection of wedge-chambered powerhouses to take its place.

Pontiac went "Wide-Track," and Chevrolet added four-door models to the top Impala lineup. Ford launched a Galaxie to rival the Impala, while Chevy turned the tables with an El Camino car-pickup to go against the Ranchero. Checker expanded beyond taxicabs, introducing a Superba passenger car.

At the small end of the scale, American Motors—focusing solely on compacts—built a record number of cars and earned a rewarding profit. Studebaker was in the throes of a comeback, courtesy of the compact Lark, a "new concept in motoring."

Analysts predicted a more stable market, courtesy of the now-required price stickers on new cars. Model-year auto output grew by 30.7 percent to more than 5.5 million. The federal gasoline tax was raised from three to four cents per gallon.

Imports enjoyed record sales, with a 62-percent increase over 1958. Shoppers could get foreign cars priced from $1048 (for a tiny Isetta) to $14,000, as the import boom went full steam ahead.

Nearly 700,000 imports were on the road as the model year began, but the total topped 1.1 million a year later.

Chrysler dealers began to sell Simcas, imported from France. In addition to the expected Volkswagens, Renaults, and Austins, buyers could choose a Berkeley, NSU Prinz, Goggomobil, or Goliath, as well as a Citroën or Hillman—even a Skoda from Czechoslovakia or a Wartburg from East Germany. This year's convention of the National Automobile Dealers Association asked the vital question: "Are imported cars here to stay?"

Unemployment eased a bit, to 5.5 percent, after the great downfall of 1958. Overall inflation actually approached zero, though new cars cost 2.6 percent more as the model year began, and the average price paid for a new automobile rose sharply (to $3150). The average used car went for just over a thousand. Despite the economic downturn, average incomes of employed workers continued to rise, nearing $4600. Physicians topped $22,000. Nearly three-fourths of families had a vehicle, but only 38 percent paid cash for one.

*Rawhide* and *Bonanza* entered TV screens for the first time, as did Rod Serling's *Twilight Zone*. Movies included *Anatomy of a Murder* with James Stewart, Billy Wilder's *Some Like It Hot*, Alfred Hitchcock's *North by Northwest*, and *On the Beach*.

In cities, at least, Americans saw more foreign films; but *Ben-Hur* would earn the best-picture Oscar. On another level, moviegoers savored such fare as *The Ghost of Dragstrip Hollow* and *Speed Crazy*.

Fidel Castro's troops moved into Havana, sending dictator Fulgencio Batista out of Cuba. Soviet leader Nikita Khrushchev toured the United States, stopping off at Disneyland—where he was denied entry for security reasons. Hawaii was admitted to the Union as the 50th state, and Charles Van Doren admitted having received answers beforehand on the popular quiz show *Twenty-One*.

Bobby Darin won a Grammy for his offbeat recording of "Mack the Knife," Johnny Mathis got "Misty," and Dion and the Belmonts warbled about "A Teenager in Love." Ace rock 'n' roller Buddy Holly was killed in a plane crash along with Ritchie Valens and The Big Bopper.

William Burroughs published *The Naked Lunch*, Norman Mailer delivered *Advertisements for Myself*, and Kurt Vonnegut issued *The Sirens of Titan*. Bestsellers included everything from *Exodus* and *Hawaii* to *The Ugly American*.

Go-carts were popular with kids and teens. Radio disc jockeys were investigated for accepting "payola" (bribes for playing certain recordings). America's first seven astronauts were selected, including John Glenn and Alan Shepard. The average person watched 42 hours' worth of TV a week.

The Automobile Manufacturers Association announced that a crankcase-ventilation device would go on cars sold in California, effective on '61 models. Before long, emissions and safety issues would change the way Americans thought about their cars and the way manufacturers built them.

Compacts would lead the way into the Sixties, followed by a fleet of mid-size models. Goliath full-size cars would not disappear for many years, and the horsepower race would gain in frenzy as "muscle cars" were added to the mix, so Americans were about to face an even wider array of automotive choices.

# 1959 Rambler

## American Motors Corporation

Rambler earns $60 million profit, building a record 374,000 automobiles

Production almost doubles in model year, as company rises to sixth place in the industry

Ambassador output grows smartly to 23,769 cars

Two-door station wagon joins Rambler American lineup; roof luggage rack is available

More than 90,000 Rambler Americans are sold, despite competition from Studebaker's new Lark series

Rambler American gets self-adjusting brakes

Ramblers use three wheelbases: 100, 108, and 117 inches

New grilles and rearranged side trim give modest facelift to middle-sized Ramblers

Separate front seats available with ten-way headrests

Six-cylinder Ramblers outsell Rebel V-8s by wide margin

Nash Metropolitans add trunk lid and wing vents

More potent Austin engine is available in Metropolitans

Metropolitan sales grow considerably—22,209 are shipped (20,435 of them to U.S.)

Among imports, Metro is second only to Volkswagen in sales—but gulf between the two is vast

1. A Rambler Ambassador Custom Country Club four-door hardtop sold for $2822, but only 1447 were built. The 327-cid V-8 made 270 horsepower. Note the pointed fins.
2. AMC built 4341 Ambassador Custom Cross Country wagons. Super versions lacked the Custom's anodized aluminum trim. 3. AMC president George Romney shows off an Ambassador Custom Country Club hardtop at corporate headquarters. 4. Ambassadors were promoted as sensibly sized, "The Modern Concept of a Luxury Car."

Who Said A Fine Car Has To Be "Big As All Outdoors"?

Ambassador by Rambler

> As a country, we may be in for some tough sledding, based on my survey of the domestic situation. We have to recognize that since World War II, our enemy has been licking the pants off us.

*American Motors president* **George Romney**, *on the American work ethic, excess consumerism, and the growth of foreign economies; May 1959*

1

2

ENTER TODAY! Win one of

# 8 RAMBLERS IN MILK-BONE SHAGGY DOG CONTEST

10,658 PRIZES WORTH $83,000

WALT DISNEY'S NEW HIT, "SHAGGY DOG"...

8 FIRST PRIZES: RAMBLER STATION WAGONS

50 2nd PRIZES: SYLVANIA 21" TV DELUXE CONSOLE MODELS

100 3rd PRIZES: SYLVANIA ALL-TRANSISTOR PORTABLE RADIOS

500 4th PRIZES: SUNBEAM AUTOMATIC ELECTRIC FRYPANS

5,000 5th PRIZES: PIONEER LADIES WALLETS

5,000 6th PRIZES: PERSONALIZED DOG FEEDING DISHES

PLUS

MILK-BONE CONTEST RULES

ENTER TODAY! MAIL THIS COUPON

5

3          4

6

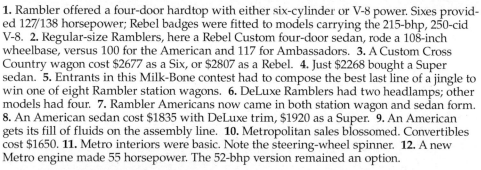

7

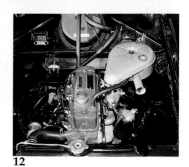

8

1. Rambler offered a four-door hardtop with either six-cylinder or V-8 power. Sixes provided 127/138 horsepower; Rebel badges were fitted to models carrying the 215-bhp, 250-cid V-8. 2. Regular-size Ramblers, here a Rebel Custom four-door sedan, rode a 108-inch wheelbase, versus 100 for the American and 117 for Ambassadors. 3. A Custom Cross Country wagon cost $2677 as a Six, or $2807 as a Rebel. 4. Just $2268 bought a Super sedan. 5. Entrants in this Milk-Bone contest had to compose the best last line of a jingle to win one of eight Rambler station wagons. 6. DeLuxe Ramblers had two headlamps; other models had four. 7. Rambler Americans now came in both station wagon and sedan form. 8. An American sedan cost $1835 with DeLuxe trim, $1920 as a Super. 9. An American gets its fill of fluids on the assembly line. 10. Metropolitan sales blossomed. Convertibles cost $1650. 11. Metro interiors were basic. Note the steering-wheel spinner. 12. A new Metro engine made 55 horsepower. The 52-bhp version remained an option.

9

10          11          12

383

## Checker Motors Corporation

Markin Body Corporation merges with Commonwealth Motors in 1921

Checker founded by Morris Markin in 1922

Early cars built in Joliet and Chicago, Illinois

Factory moves to Kalamazoo, Michigan, in 1923

Cars initially use four-cylinder engines; inline sixes and eights are added later

First passenger model, the Checker Utility, offered in 1931-32

Prewar Checkers are changed regularly in design to keep up with contemporary trends

First postwar civilian model, the Superba, released in 1959

Superba based on the A8 taxi introduced in 1956.

Superba gets quad headlights in place of the A8's duals

Power is provided by a 226-cid Continental inline six similar to that used in the Kaiser/Frazer

Engine offered in two versions: L-head with 80 horsepower, overhead-valve model with 122 bhp

Four-door sedan and four-door wagon offered, each in standard or Special trim

Markin promises not to initiate change for the sake of change; indeed, cars continue 1956 styling to the bitter end

1

2

3

**1-3.** "Taxi tough" Checker sedans rode a 120-inch wheelbase and tipped the scales at around 3400 pounds—about the same as a Chevrolet Biscayne—while wagons weighed nearly 400 pounds more. Sedans started at $2542, wagons at $2896; both about $250 more than the cheapest comparable Chevy. The 80-horsepower Continental L-head six had a 7.3:1 compression ratio that let it run on poor-quality gas, but most cars had the no-cost overhead-valve option with 8.0:1 compression and 122 bhp. Interiors were Spartan with rubber floor mats and cardboard headliners. The model name switched to Marathon in the early '60s and Chevy engines were used after 1964, but the cars changed little otherwise through their final season in 1982. Civilian production rarely exceeded 1000 per year.

# Chrysler Corporation

Chrysler budgets $150 million for the '59 models—much of which goes to Plymouth

Swivel semi-bucket front seats are standard on Chrysler 300-E, optional on other makes/models

Chryslers are powered by 383- and 413-cid wedge V-8 engines; legendary Hemis are gone

Chrysler 300-E boasts 380 horsepower from 413-cid V-8; production drops to 690 cars

Chrysler output rises slightly, due largely to Windsor sedans

DeSoto sales continue to sag

Midyear brings Seville editions to mark DeSoto's 30th year

Final year for Dodge/Plymouth L-head six-cylinder engine

Plymouths are sold by Dodge dealers for the last time

New electronic rear-view mirror cuts glare when a headlight beam hits its surface

Rear air suspensions available; speed warnings also optional

Stainless steel roof sections available for Imperial hardtops

Plymouth Plaza gone; Savoy is now the base model

Plymouth finishes third, followed by Pontiac and Olds

Chrysler dealers now sell French Simca

1

2

3

4

**1-2.** Just 286 open Chrysler New Yorkers went to buyers, at $4890. Taillights were new. So was the 413-cid V-8 developing 350 horsepower. This convertible has the new Autronic Eye headlight dimmer. **3.** Chrysler's '59 facelift included a blunted front with a simpler grille. New Yorker four-door hardtops started at $4533, with 4805 built. Backup lights became standard. Note the distinctive two-toning. **4.** Adding a quart of oil was a regular event, even in a New Yorker. Sunoco stations delivered six grades of fuel from a single pump.

# 1959 Chrysler

1

2

3

4

6

1. Chrysler Windsors got a new Golden Lion 383-cid V-8 promising 305 horses. This hardtop has an optional two-tone roof. Spring action swung the extra-cost swivel seat outward; body motion glided it back. 2. Chrysler's 300-E kept its distinctive grille. Only 550 coupes were produced. 3. Responding to demand for a cheaper convertible, a $3620 ragtop joined the Windsor series. 4. Output of the open 300-E came to just 140 cars. 5. Chief engineer Bob Rodger inspects the new dual-quad 413-cid V-8 in a 300-E. This "wedge" V-8 weighed 101 pounds less than a Hemi and delivered the same 380 horsepower. Hydraulic lifters were new. 6. The Brooks Stevens-designed Scimitar employed a Chrysler chassis and running gear under its aluminum body. Three were built. 7. Restyled "lion-hearted" Chryslers had channeled roofs separated by a stainless-steel band.

NEW CHRYSLER '59

... the lion-hearted car that's every inch a new adventure

LION-HEARTED
CHRYSLER '59

7

5

1

2

3

1. Once again, the Adventurer served as DeSoto's most invigorating model. Only 590 coupes were produced, along with a mere 97 convertibles. 2. A Firedome four-door sedan started at $3234. Ornate styling was most evident up front, led by a two-section bumper and new grille. 3. Mid-range Firedome interiors seemed inviting, but the faltering DeSotos looked too much like Chryslers—and cost nearly as much. 4. A new 383-cid V-8 with dual four-barrel carburetors entered Adventurers, yielding 350 horsepower. 5. Less-potent renditions of the 383-cid engine powered Firedome (shown) and Fireflite models.

> 66 DeSoto is looking forward to a rising long-range demand for its cars. 99
>
> *DeSoto general manager*
> **J. B. Wagstaff**; *March 1959*

4

5

1

2

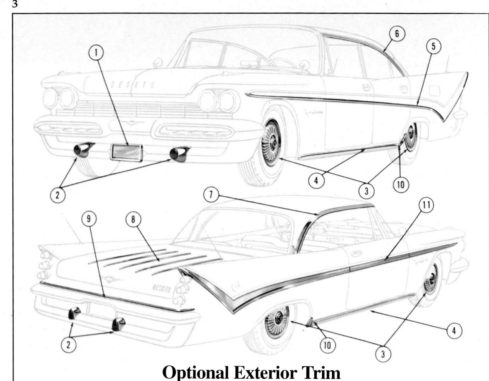

3

**CHRYSLER CORPORATION SWIVEL SEAT**
DESIGN AND OPERATION

PULL-DOWN
CENTER ARMREST

CENTER
SEAT

SPRING

RELEASE LEVER

*RIDING
POSITION*

PIVOT

ROLLER
TRACK

NYLON
ROLLERS

*ENTRY – EXIT
POSITION*

**1.** Nine-passenger Explorer station wagons came in both the Fireflite and Firesweep series, with an $850 price difference. **2.** Optional swivel seats rotated outward to a 40-degree angle. **3.** The extensive options list allowed a DeSoto to be customized to its owner's taste. **4.** Hundreds of towns looked at least a bit like Murphysboro, Illinois, as pictured from the courthouse steps. Note the $2 hotel rooms. Before the advent of major discount chains, small department stores occupied many a downtown corner.

## Optional Exterior Trim

| | | | |
|---|---|---|---|
| **1.** | License plate frame | **6.** | Roof moulding |
| **2.** | Rubber-tipped | | (4 door sedan) |
| | bumper guards | **7.** | Roof moulding |
| **3.** | Wheel covers | | (2 door Sportsman) |
| **4.** | Sill mouldings | **8.** | Deck lid accent stripes |
| **5.** | Color sweep moulding | | |

| | |
|---|---|
| **9.** | Lower rear deck |
| | panel moulding |
| **10.** | Stone shield |
| **11.** | Anodized aluminum |
| | insert |

4

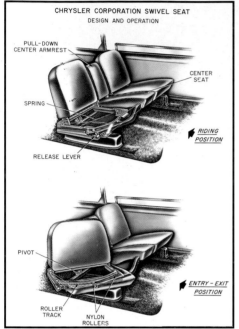

1

2

3

4

5

1-2. A luxurious Dodge Custom Royal Lancer hardtop coupe started at $3201, with 6278 built. This one has the 383-cid D-500 engine, but a Ram-Fire 361 was standard. A comparable Coronet cost $437 less and outsold the Custom Royal Lancer by more than three to one. 3. Drivers needed to do more than push buttons, but they faced a new elliptical steering wheel and color-coded speedometer, as well as the TorqueFlite control panel. 4. Six-window styling marked the $3145 Custom Royal four-door sedan, of which 8925 were produced. 5. This Regal Lancer hardtop might have been the successor to the fancy 1958 Special of that name. Sadly, the proposal was scuttled in April 1958 due to Chrysler's financial ills. The prototype wore unique bodyside moldings with inserts, special roof trim, and other styling deviations.

1

The Swing-Out Seat that says..."Please Come In"

'59 DODGE

3

2

4

5

**1-2.** Production of the Dodge Custom Royal Lancer convertible, starting at $3422, dropped a bit to 984 cars. This Canary Yellow ragtop sports twin rear antennas ahead of the tacky-look tailfins, as well as a six-way power seat with swivel operation. Underhood sat Dodge's 383-cid, 345-horsepower Super D-500 dual-quad engine with a high-lift cam. **3.** More than 16,000 Dodge buyers accepted the invitation and paid $70.95 for Swing-Out Swivel Seats. **4.** As you swung your legs into the car, the swivel seat followed and locked into position. **5.** With swivel seating, the center section was fixed in place for three-passenger occupancy—or it folded down as a central armrest. **6.** Some deemed the latest Dodges garish—a virtual caricature of 1957-58 styling, exemplified by the exaggerated fins and Jet-Trail taillights in chrome-bezel tubes. Despite such criticism, shoppers took kindly to the new Dodges. Output rose 13 percent, moving the division up to eighth place in the industry.

6

**1.** With a fresh front end aiming to impart a sense of motion, the Imperial Crown Southampton hardtop sold about as well as the lower-priced Custom. **2.** Base Imperials got a Custom badge. **3.** A Custom sedan cost $5016, as did the more popular hardtop sedan. **4.** An Imperial Crown sedan brought $5647. **5.** Both the LeBaron Southampton hardtop and pillared sedan listed at $6103. **6.** Imperial styling had never been more distinct from other Chrysler makes. **7.** Imperials adopted a 413-cid V-8, belting out 350 horsepower. **8-9.** Ghia continued to issue Crown Imperial Limousines—seven this year—with a $15,075 price tag and 149.5-inch wheelbase. Weighing almost three tons, the luxury boat stuck with the Hemi V-8. Each had a division window, jump seats, and padded rear roof. **10.** Britain's Queen Elizabeth II and Prince Philip greeted crowds from a special Imperial.

> 66 Had it not been for the steel scarcity, we would have had the best fourth quarter in Imperial history. 99
>
> *Chrysler and Imperial general manager* **C. E. Briggs***; December 1959*

# 1959 Plymouth

1

2

4

5

3

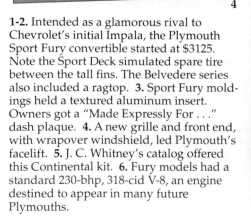

6

**1-2.** Intended as a glamorous rival to Chevrolet's initial Impala, the Plymouth Sport Fury convertible started at $3125. Note the Sport Deck simulated spare tire between the tall fins. The Belvedere series also included a ragtop. **3.** Sport Fury moldings held a textured aluminum insert. Owners got a "Made Expressly For . . ." dash plaque. **4.** A new grille and front end, with wrapover windshield, led Plymouth's facelift. **5.** J. C. Whitney's catalog offered this Continental kit. **6.** Fury models had a standard 230-bhp, 318-cid V-8, an engine destined to appear in many future Plymouths.

1

2

3

4

**1-2.** A 260-bhp, 318-cid V-8 was standard under Sport Fury hoods, but many got a Golden Commando 361-cid V-8 that produced 305 horsepower. Hardtops began at $2927. Swivel buckets were standard. **3.** George J. Huebner Jr. (*left*), executive engineer in charge of research, and engineering vice president Paul C. Ackerman, examine the experimental Turbine Special at Chrysler's Engineering Building. Running on diesel fuel in this Fury, the engine achieved 19.39 mpg on a 576-mile run from Toledo, Ohio, to Woodbridge, New Jersey. **4.** Top-selling Plymouth was the $2283 Savoy sedan, with 84,272 going to buyers. **5.** Sport Suburban wagons served in the 'burbs and the great outdoors, hauling six or nine passengers. **6.** Disappearing rear windows in station wagons could be controlled from the driver's seat.

5

6

393

# 1959 Edsel

## Ford Motor Company

Wrapover windshields offer greater glass area

Edsel line includes only Ranger, Corsair, and Villager wagon

All-new engines go into Edsels, including six-cylinder; big 410-cid V-8 is deleted

Edsel now aims at lowest segment of medium-priced field

Edsel drops to 14th in industry

Edsel ceases production in November 1959

Conservative, squared-off Ford design wins styling award at Brussels World's Fair

Ford choices include 332- and 352-cid V-8s with up to 300 bhp—or even a rare 430-cid engine

Luxury Galaxie series with Thunderbird-style roof joins Ford in mid-season, and accounts for 27 percent of production

Ford output rises 47 percent—almost ties Chevrolet for Number One in sales

Ford Thunderbirds can have huge 430-cid Lincoln V-8

Continental is no longer a separate marque from Lincoln

Continental Mark IV line includes Town Car and limousine

Mercury is longer and more sculpted; Turnpike Cruiser gone

1

2

3

4

1-2. Edsel's sole convertible came in the Corsair series. Only 1343 were produced. Corsairs got a new 225-horsepower, 332-cid V-8, but $58 more bought a 303-horse, 361-cid V-8. **3.** Buying an Edsel seemed to make very *good* sense to some shoppers, but the die was cast for the car's quick demise. Essentially reskinned Fords, all Edsels now rode a 120-inch wheelbase. **4.** Shorter dimensions allowed Edsel to advertise easier parking. **5.** Evening wear in an Edsel? Why not? This Corsair four-door hardtop listed at $2885.

5

1

> "History's greatest year for imported autos has come to an end and there are indications that never again will the U.S. market for foreign cars be so fat."
>
> *Journalist* **Robert M. Lienert**, Automotive News *story; January 1959*

2

3

4

**EDSEL FUNERAL SALE**

**YOU ARE INVITED TO VIEW THE FINAL REMAINS OF THE EDSEL**

(IT DIED, YOU KNOW)

JIM BARNETT LINCOLN-MERCURY, is preparing to bury the EDSEL. There are not to the "bone to their burial expense.

This is your opportunity to save $ $ $ $. While you're here, take a peek at the BETTER IDEA cars from Ford!

DON'T SEND FLOWERS BUT COME SAVE $ $ $

**JIM BARNETT LINCOLN-MERCURY**
(GERMAN FORD) **TAUNUS** (M.P.G.)

**BIG FUNERAL SALE! SAVE $ $ $**
500 MONTGOMERY ST.                 A.Dams 3-3054

## The Last Rites

Jim Barnett Lincoln-Mercury in Savannah, GA, ran this ad in the *Savannah News*. Barnett also placed a black pine coffin in front of his dealership to mark the demise of the Edsel. "Here Lies the Edsel!" was painted in white letters on the coffin, which was flanked by two Edsels. Prices of the dealer's remaining Edsels were slashed in line with the "funeral services."

**1.** Edsel Rangers, including this $2691 hardtop, carried a new 292-cid V-8 that made 200 horsepower; a 145-bhp six could be installed instead. Just 5474 were produced. **2.** Top Edsel seller was the $2684 Ranger four-door sedan, with 12,814 rolling off the line. **3.** This Ranger two-door sedan's top claim to fame is the name of its owner: Edsel Ford—not related to the Ford Motor Company family. Edsel output totaled 44,891 cars. **4.** Nine-passenger Villager station wagons easily outsold their six-seat companions. **5.** A Villager wagon and Corsair hardtop matched dimensions at the Ford Proving Grounds.

# 1959 Ford

1

2

3

6

4

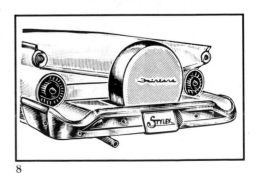

5

1. Until the new Galaxie series arrived at midyear, Fairlane 500 was the top model. Ford issued 23,892 Victoria two-door hard-tops, at $2537. Ford called its '59s "the world's most beautifully proportioned cars." 2-3. Galaxie Club Sedans started at $2528 and sold well. Ford's outer body panels were new, and much of the inner structure revised, on a 118-inch wheelbase. Taillights reverted to round shape. 4. Economy got a big push in ads, along with roominess—big enough for a man wearing a fedora and his daughter wielding a hula-hoop. 5. Almost 46,000 Ford fans got their hands on a Galaxie Sunliner, which started at $2839. 6. Convertible dashboards matched the body. Windshields curved at the top, for 29-percent more glass area. 7. Workers guide a sedan body onto its chassis. 8. Naturally, Fairlanes could get a Continental kit from J. C. Whitney catalog.

7

8

# Sail Through Tower Bridge

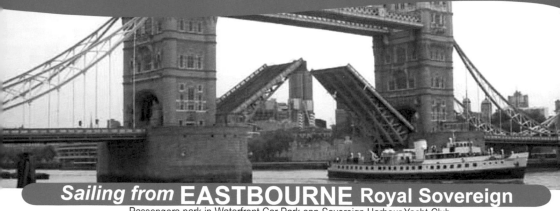

## Sailing from EASTBOURNE Royal Sovereign

Passengers park in Waterfront Car Park opp Sovereign Harbour Yacht Club
Assemble at the blue gates opp Sovereign Harbour Yacht Club where shuttle bus takes you to board Balmoral

### SAIL THROUGH TOWER BRIDGE

**MONDAY JUNE 29 Leave 9am** back 9.30pm

Day Cruise to London – sail round Dungeness - North Foreland – and cruise up the Thames to the heart of London. See Thames Flood Barrier - magnificent Greenwich Waterfront - famous Clipper Ship Cutty Sark – Millennium Dome – Canary Wharf & see Tower Bridge open for you to sail through. With views of Tower of London & HMS Belfast join your inclusive coach home £39.95 SC £37.95.

## Sailing from RYE Wharf

Free Car Parking at Rye Harbour Car Park - Allow 10mins to walk to Wharf

### SAIL THROUGH TOWER BRIDGE

**FRIDAY JULY 3 Leave 9am** back 9.30pm

Don't miss the only sailing from Rye aboard Balmoral in 2009. Magnificent Day Cruise to London – sail round Dungeness - North Foreland – and cruise up the Thames to the heart of London. See Thames Flood Barrier - magnificent Greenwich Waterfront - famous Clipper Ship Cutty Sark – Millennium Dome – Canary Wharf & see Tower Bridge open for you to sail through. With views of Tower of London & HMS Belfast turn in the Pool of London and sail to Greeniwch to join your inclusive coach for Rye £39.95 SENIOR CITIZENS £37.95.

*Paddle Steamer Waverley* sails on the South Coast of England and the Thames in September & October - Find out more & book online or call for a brochure.

# CHILDREN Under 18 Half Fare - Under 5 Free

# DISCOUNTS for GROUPS of 10 or more

## BE SURE OF YOUR TICKETS BOOK ONLINE AT
## www.waverleyexcursions.co.uk

## or book by credit or debit card by calling 0845 130 4647

When booking by phone your ticket will be posted to you or if time is short will be available for you to collect on board. *You can also buy tickets from* TOURIST INFORMATION CENTRES at Bournemouth, Bridport, Christchurch, Eastbourne, Hayling Island, Hastings, Lyme Regis, Portsmouth, Southampton, Southsea, Wimborne, & All Isle of Wight Tourist Information Centre

**Gift Aid It!** If you are a UK taxpayer we can claim an extra 25% from the Taxman to help preserve these historic ships so that your kids and grandkids can enjoy a sail in years to come! Your fare includes a voluntary 10% donation You don't have to do anything - we'll make the claim! *E.g Fare £25.41 Voluntary Donation £2.54 Total Fare £27.95*

Waverley Steam Navigation Co. Limited, Waverley Terminal, 36 Lancefield Quay, Glasgow G3 8HA
A Charity Registered in Scotland SC005832 On Board Services provided by Waverley Excursions Ltd

All bookings are taken, tickets issued & all passengers & others carried subject to the Terms & Conditions of Waverley Excursions Ltd. Copies available on request from the company's offices or on demand from the Purser at the gangway before going on board. All sailings are subject to weather, visibility & circumstances permitting. Catering offered subject to availability. An alternative ship may be provided or any sailings, routes or destinations may be altered, if weather conditions make this necessary. No passenger under the influence of alcohol will be allowed to board the ship & no alcohol may be brought on board. No refunds can be made for tickets purchased for sailings that take place, but unused tickets can be used, up to their purchase value towards any alternative sailing. Passengers are entitled to a full refund for the value of any tickets booked for a sailing that is cancelled or can retain the ticket for use on any other sailing at no extra charge.

# Step Aboard
## for a Great Day Out!

**Discover the Jurassic Coast - Cruise round the Isle of Wight & Sail all the way to London and Through Tower Bridge!**

BALMORAL

*Sailing from* **Bridport♦Bournemouth♦Southampton♦Portsmouth Yarmouth♦Ryde♦Cowes♦Worthing♦Eastbourne♦Rye**

**ON BOARD: Self Service Restaurant ● Lounges ● Souvenir Shop**

# Find out more & Book Online @
# www.waverleyexcursions.co.uk

1. Wearing a fresh horizontal-themed grille, Thunderbird convertibles listed for $3979. Output soared past the 10,000 mark. The automatic top was stowed completely out of sight. 2. T-Bird hardtops were near-duplicates of '58, but volume rose to 57,195 cars. Buyers could now order Lincoln's 350-horsepower, 430-cid V-8 instead of the 300-bhp, 352-cid engine. 3. Ranchero car-pickups were based on big Fords for the last time. Interiors compared to a Country Sedan's. 4. Optional air suspension helped keep a Country Sedan on an even keel, regardless of the load inside. 5. Campers could survive almost indefinitely with all that gear packed in—and on—this wood-grain-trimmed Country Squire wagon. 6. The Skokie, Illinois, fire department employed Ford Country Sedan station wagons—and Mack fire trucks.

" We have tried to learn the business and have learned one thing the hard way: It was our business and no one gave a tinker's dam whether we won or lost. "

*Houston, Mississippi, Ford dealer **Harry J. Vickery**, on small dealers' struggles with manufacturers and political legislation; May 1959*

1

2

❝And boy, does Lincoln-Mercury seem to be scared of the small cars coming next year. From all I can see, everybody in the medium-priced line is scared as hell, but they won't admit it. I don't know what's going to happen, but it can't be much worse than this year. ❞

**Unidentified Lincoln-Mercury dealer,** *on 1959 model-year sales and the small American cars set to bow for 1960; July 1959*

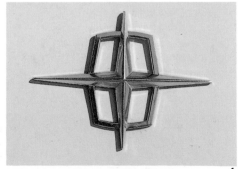

4

1-2. Lincoln's Continental Mark IV series included this $6845 four-door hardtop, plus a hardtop coupe, pillared sedan, and convertible. Defying recent trends, Lincoln's 430-cid V-8 dropped to 350 bhp. **3.** All instruments sat ahead of the Continental driver, who faced an upright-looking dash. Upholstery conveyed subtle elegance. **4.** Billed as the "world's most admired car," Continentals featured a reverse-sloped, retractable back window.

3

**1.** Hess & Eisenhardt, an Ohio specialty coachbuilder, turned the Continental Mark IV into a divider-window Limousine with a $10,230 sticker. The company also issued a $9208 Town Car, with the same padded landau-style roof and tiny rear privacy windows. Stately interiors in leather and gray broadcloth imparted a conservative demeanor, but held plenty of amenities. Finished only in Presidential Black, these formal machines were built in small numbers: 49 limos and 78 Town Cars. **2.** A Lincoln Capri four-door hardtop cost $5090, as did the slower-selling pillared sedan. Premieres came in the same body styles. Lincoln had its own grille texture, but shared front-end changes with Continental. Ads pushed classic beauty, craftsmanship, prestige—plus "sheer elegance." **3.** Ford car/truck chief Robert S. McNamara (*center*) looks pleased with the corporation's full '59 line: Ford, Thunderbird, Edsel, Lincoln, and Mercury.

# 1959 Mercury

1

**Makes you feel good just looking at it, or sitting in it**

**'59 MERCURY**
*Planned for People*

2

3

4

**1.** Wrapover windshields gave Mercury 60-percent more glass area. Each model displayed a fresh grille and restyled trim. Mercury issued 6713 Montclair four-door hardtops, starting at $3437 with a 322-horsepower, 383-cid V-8 engine. **2.** Economy got more emphasis, though Mercury ads focused mainly on the joys of driving a spacious convertible. The monstrous 400-horsepower engine option was gone. **3.** A Colony Park station wagon seated six and started at $3932, with 5929 built. Note the woodgrain trim. Transmission tunnels shrunk in size for more legroom, accomplished by moving the engine and wheels forward. **4.** Toll booths weren't yet common, but appeared here and there. This one stood along the Turner Turnpike between Oklahoma City and Tulsa.

1

2

3

**1.** Top-of-the-line Mercury was once again the Park Lane, its 430-cid V-8 engine detuned to 345 horsepower. Convertibles cost $4206—1254 were built. **2.** A Park Lane two-door hardtop went for $3955, with 4060 produced. **3.** Longer and roomier this year, with a lowered hood, Mercs weren't quite as lively as before but managed to exude luxury for a moderate entry fee. **4.** Drive-in movies had existed since 1933 and continued to draw crowds—both whole families and just teens, most often in couples and groups. Cartoons and coming attractions typically preceded the feature movies, as at this Gary, Indiana, outdoor theater.

4

> **"** The factory just ain't building many lower-priced units. **"**
>
> **Unidentified California new-car dealer,** *lamenting the paucity of American "economy" models desired by recession-scarred buyers; February 1959*

# 1959 Buick

## General Motors Corporation

Four-door hardtops get flat roofs and "picture window" wraparound back glass

Buick line is renamed: LeSabre, Invicta, Electra, Electra 225

Buicks wear "delta-wing" canted fins, which are reflected in front-end shape

Buicks offer new 401-cid V-8

Buick drops from fifth to seventh in production race

Cadillacs carry new 390-cid V-8 and wear towering fins

Eldorados no longer display unique tail treatment

Bigger Chevrolet body flaunts "batwing" rear deck—far more radical than this year's Ford

Chevrolet's 119-inch wheelbase is the longest yet

Impala is now a full top-of-the-line Chevrolet series, sending Bel Air down a notch; Pontiac's Bonneville series also expands

Chevrolets can have close-ratio four-speed manual

Chevrolet finishes first again, with output up 28 percent—but Ford nips at its heels . . . both makes top 1.4 million cars

Oldsmobiles have Air-Scoop flanged brake drums for quicker cooling and less fade

Pontiac introduces split-grille design and Wide-Track stance

1

2

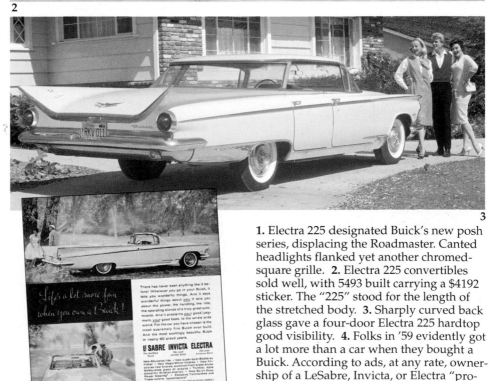

3

4

1. Electra 225 designated Buick's new posh series, displacing the Roadmaster. Canted headlights flanked yet another chromed-square grille. 2. Electra 225 convertibles sold well, with 5493 built carrying a $4192 sticker. The "225" stood for the length of the stretched body. 3. Sharply curved back glass gave a four-door Electra 225 hardtop good visibility. 4. Folks in '59 evidently got a lot more than a car when they bought a Buick. According to ads, at any rate, ownership of a LeSabre, Invicta, or Electra "proclaims your good judgment, your good taste [and] says wonderful things about you." This year's Buick was "so new," said General Manager Edward T. Ragsdale, that "it had to have new series names."

1

❝Our dealers could have delivered five times as many if they had them in stock.❞

*Buick general manager* **Edward T. Ragsdale**, *on good early sales figures for the 1959 Buick line; September 1958*

2

3

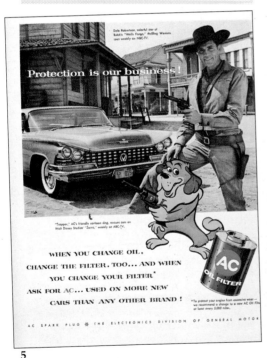

5

4

6

**1.** LeSabre was billed as "the thriftiest Buick," Invicta "the most spirited." This LeSabre hardtop cost $2849. **2.** LeSabres got a 364-cid V-8, rated 250 bhp. Buick issued 10,489 LeSabre convertibles, at $3129. **3.** This LeSabre hardtop sedan shows off its wraparound rear window. **4.** Buick's bread-and-butter model was the LeSabre sedan, with 51,379 produced. **5.** AC advised an oil-filter change every 5000 miles. TV gunslinger Dale Robertson starred in the Buick-sponsored *Wells Fargo* series. **6.** An Electra 225 paced the Indy 500 race, won by Rodger Ward.

1

2

3

4

> 66 Cadillacs are nine inches longer this year and they are so long and so wide that we would have to rebuild our ramps to accommodate them. 99
>
> *St. Louis City Auto Parks vice-president* **Wayne Stedelin**, *on his firm's instruction to its attendants not to accept 1959 Cadillacs for parking; October 1958*

**1-2.** Eldorados lost their unique tail treatment and wheels. Both the Biarritz convertible and Seville hardtop cost $7401. Output totaled 1320 and 975 cars, respectively. **3.** Both Eldos wore wider upper-body chrome moldings, plus block lettering on front fenders. Air suspensions proved to be leak-prone. The enlarged 390-cid V-8 delivered 345 horsepower under Eldorado hoods—an all-time peak for rear-drive Eldos. **4-5.** An Eldorado Brougham four-door hardtop wore different fins than other models—a design that would go on all 1960 Cadillacs. Just 99 were built this year, priced at $13,075. Broughams were the first Cadillacs to oust the Panoramic windshield. Dashboards held less chrome, and interiors were a little less lavish, lacking the prior perfume bottles and silver cups. With a 130-inch wheelbase, like most Cadillacs, space was roomy in the rear. Broughams now were built at the Pinin Farina plant in Turin, Italy.

5

*Cadillac*...world's best synonym for quality!

> **"** Big cars will stay in the fore-front. **"**

*Cadillac general manager*
**James M. Roche**, *on increasing buyer interest in small cars; March 1959*

**1.** Critics faulted Cadillac's wild fins, but the public liked them. Rear side windows were fixed on hardtop sedans. **2.** To most people, Cadillac still stood for quality. **3.** A Series 62 hardtop went for $4892, but the fancier Coupe de Ville cost $5252. **4.** In addition to the six-window Sedan de Ville, Cadillac offered a four-window model. **5.** More than 11,000 buyers paid $5455 for a Series 62 ragtop. **6.** Doors on the Cyclone show car slid to the rear as the dome opened. Nose cones contained radar.

# 1959 Chevrolet

> **❝**It will be a completely new car and not a derivative of any previous models.**❞**

*General Motors Technical Center technical director* **Dr. Peter Kyropoulos**, *on GM's upcoming Corvair; May 1959*

**1-2.** Impala Sport hardtops and ragtops commanded attention, but Impala was now a full series. With a V-8, the coupe listed at $2717, but a six-cylinder version saved $118. **3.** Impala interiors exhibited their top-of-the-line status. **4.** Base V-8, for an Impala or any model, was the carryover 283-cid version with 185 horsepower. Ratings up to 290 bhp were available—or a 348-cid V-8 could be installed with as many as 315 horses. **5.** An Impala convertible cost $2967 with V-8 power. **6.** Fender skirts and a Continental kit might come from the factory—or the J. C. Whitney catalog.

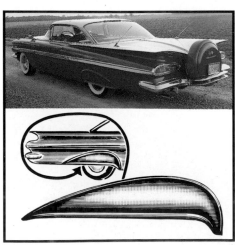

NOTHING'S NEW
LIKE CHEVY'S NEW!

CHEVROLET

1. Corvette production hit 9670 cars. The standard 283-cid V-8 made 230 bhp with options to 290. New trailing radius rods helped during hard acceleration. 2. A new El Camino car-pickup carried an 1150-pound load. 3. With a V-8, a Parkwood wagon cost $2867. Chevrolet also had Brookwood, Kingswood, and Nomad wagons. 4. Plenty of Bel Air sedans held the 235-cid six. 5. Not everyone called Chevy's deck "saucy" or its grille "elegant." 6. Danger! Hanging onto a Chevrolet to pick up speed was not a wise move. 7. A front end takes shape as its fenders and grille drop into position. 8. That Chevy's driver could have stopped at the Orange Julius stand while awaiting a $1.25 wash.

# 1959 Oldsmobile

1

2

3

4

5

6

**1.** Super 88 and Ninety-Eight Oldsmobiles earned a bored-out 394-cid V-8 making 315 bhp. This low-slung Ninety-Eight Scenic hardtop cost $4086. Lengths grew ten inches as part of the "Linear Look." **2-3.** Top-selling Olds Ninety-Eight was the Holiday hardtop sedan. Note the huge expanse of back glass. **4.** Occupants gained four inches of shoulder room. Options included a Safety Sentinel and Autronic Eye. **5.** An Olds Ninety-Eight sedan went for $3890. Lower-body sheetmetal was fuller, atop a stronger, wider Guard-Beam chassis. **6.** Visibility improved via the new Vista-Panoramic windshield.

### First Daytona 500— February 22, 1959

In the final lap of this historic event (*upper left*) at the new Daytona International Speedway, Lee Petty in Oldsmobile number 42 vies for the lead with Johnny Beauchamp. After a photo finish, Beauchamp and his Thunder-bird went to Victory Circle. However, four days later (*above*), judges changed their minds and NASCAR head Bill France, Sr., awarded a trophy to Petty.

1. A thin-section roofline is evident in the $3328 Super 88 Scenicoupe. Oldsmobile called its '59s "the most distinctively different models in our 61-year history." 2. Dynamic 88 models got a 371-cid V-8 engine with 270 or 300 horsepower. 3. A sectioned panel made the Super 88 dash look immense. 4. A roll-down rear window eased access to the cargo area of a Super 88 Fiesta wagon. 5. Print ads promoted coming TV programs, such as Bing Crosby's golf tournament sponsored by Oldsmobile. 6. Shoppers in Louisville, Kentucky, might have bought an Olds at this dealership.

# 1959 Pontiac

1

“We have placed more emphasis on the sculpturing of sheetmetal, less on bright work.”

*Pontiac general manager* **Semon E. Knudsen**, *on the 1959 Pontiac line; August 1958*

2

**1-2.** One of four Bonneville body styles, the $3257 two-door hardtop was outsold by the Vista hardtop sedan. **3.** New Wide-Track engineering increased tread width by nearly five inches, greatly improving stability. Pontiac's claim to have "broken all bonds of traditional styling and engineering" turned out to be valid. **4.** Bonnevilles contained plenty of dashboard brightwork, along with colorful upholstery. **5.** Crisply styled on all-new bodies and introducing the split-grille theme that would become its trademark, the '59s established the pattern for Pontiac performance in the Sixties. Wide-Track Pontiacs really did rank among the most roadable American cars. **6.** Bonneville production included 11,426 convertibles, which listed for $3478. Seats were trimmed with leather and jewel-tone Morrokide, with buckets optional.

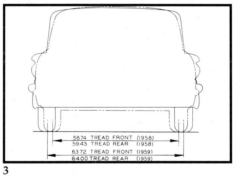

3

4

5

6

410

1

2

3

**1.** Pontiac Catalinas rode a 122-inch wheelbase, two inches shorter than the Star Chief and Bonneville. **2.** Catalina models included a two-door hardtop. **3.** Top seller was the Catalina sedan. This year's V-8 made 245 to 345 horsepower, though a 215-bhp economy engine was also available. **4.** Dealers issued promotional postcards. This Pontiac store served the Camden, New Jersey, area. **5.** Superior Coach Corp. marketed this Cargo Cruiser on a Pontiac chassis, with a stretched 148-inch wheelbase. Priced at $7775, it promised 50 percent more cargo space than a wagon.

5

4

# Studebaker-Packard Corporation

Compact Lark introduced—with perfect timing

Lark two-doors and four-doors are built on 108.5-inch wheelbase; wagons ride a 113-inch wheelbase

Body styles include four-door sedan, two-door sedan and wagon, and two-door hardtop

"Standard" Studebakers and the Golden Hawk hardtop coupe are dropped; only the Silver Hawk pillared coupe carries on from '58

Despite fewer model offerings, Studebaker sales skyrocket

Production increases by over 150 percent thanks to new Lark compact—and, oddly, the nation's economic recession

Larks carry dual headlights while most cars have quad headlights

Larks boast large, square grille similar to Hawks

Packards are history, though the name remains in the corporate title

All six-cylinder Larks and Hawks are powered by de-stroked 169.6-cid engine making 90 horsepower; Larks so equipped are designated Lark VI

Eight-cylinder Larks (designated Lark VIII) and Hawks get a 259.2-cid V-8 making 180 or 195 horsepower

Larger 289-cid V-8 from '58 is dropped

1

2

3

> 66 It's the only passenger car I have ever driven that has the feel and handling of a sports car. It's very stabilized, very solid. 99
>
> *Laguna Beach, California, Studebaker dealer* **Frank M. Darling**, *on Studebaker's "Model X" small car, which debuted for 1959 as the Lark; August 1958*

**1.** Released during an economic recession, the compact Lark replaced Studebaker's standard line—and more than doubled the company's sales. Six-cylinder models, called Lark VI, brought back the smaller 169.6-cid L-head six last used in '54, now making 90 horsepower. Prices started at $1925 for a DeLuxe two-door sedan. This upscale Regal hardtop coupe sold for $2275 as a six, $2411 with a V-8. **2-3.** Eight-cylinder Larks carried a Lark VIII designation, signifying a 259-cid V-8 with 180 standard horsepower or 195 with the Power Pack. Opting for the V-8 added only about $135 to a Lark's price, but it was available only with Regal trim. In these economy-conscious times, sixes outsold eights by a wide margin.

1

2

3

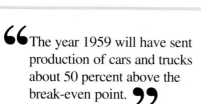

4

5

6

7

> 66 The year 1959 will have sent production of cars and trucks about 50 percent above the break-even point. 99
>
> *Studebaker-Packard Corp. president **Harold E. Churchill**, on S-P's $20 million profit for the model year; September 1959*

1-3. Lark wagons came only in two-door versions for '59. Offered in DeLuxe or Regal trim with six-cylinder or V-8 power, they rode a longer wheelbase than other Larks, 113 inches versus 108.5. **4.** These '59 Larks are nearing the end of Studebaker's assembly line in South Bend, Indiana. **5.** Leo Newman and Nathan Altman, partners in this South Bend dealership, later went on to buy the rights to build Studebaker's Avanti coupe . **6.** The state of Indiana bought 35 Studebakers for government service. **7.** Silver Hawks offered the same engine choices as Larks, but Hawk V-8s outsold six-cylinder counterparts. **8-9.** Hawk interiors looked sporty with rolled upholstery and tooled metal trim.

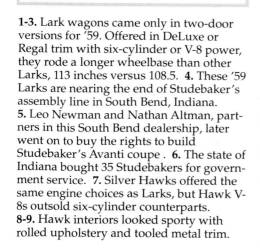

8

9

# INDEX